NORTH INTO FREEDOM

NORTH INTO FREEDOM

The Autobiography
of John Malvin,
Free Negro,
1795 - 1880

*Edited and with
an Introduction by
ALLAN PESKIN*

THE WESTERN RESERVE HISTORICAL SOCIETY
Cleveland, Ohio

THE WERNER D. MUELLER REPRINT SERIES

Works Translated From German: Completed
Jacob Mueller. *Memories of a Forty-Eighter* (1896)

Works Translated From German: In Process
Cleveland and Its Germans (1897-98 edition)
Cleveland and Its Germans (1907 edition)
Waechter und Anzeiger Jubilee Edition (1902)

Reprints of Significant Local Titles: Completed
Eric Johannesen. *Cleveland Architecture, 1876-1976* (1979)
John Malvin. *North Into Freedom* (1879, 1988)

Reprints of Significant Local Titles: In Process
Edmund H. Chapman. *Cleveland: Village to Metropolis* (1964,1981)

© 1996 by Allan Peskin
All rights reserved
Library of Congress Catalog Card Number 87-29845
ISBN 0-911704-48-5
Manufactured in the United States of America

Published in 1966 by The Press of Western Reserve University
Reprinted in 1988 by The Kent State University Press

Library of Congress Cataloging-in-Publication Data

Malvin, John, 1795-1880
  North into freedom.

  Reprint. Originally published: Autobiography of
John Malvin. Cleveland : Leader Print. Co., 1879.
  Bibliography: p.
  Incudes index.
  1. Malvin, John, 1795-1880. 2. Afro-Americans —
Ohio — Biography. 3. Afro-Americans — Civil rights —
Ohio. 4. Ohio — Biography. 5. Afro-Americans — Ohio —
History — 19th century. 6. Ohio — Race relations.
  7. Ohio — History — 1787-1865. I. Peskin, Allan.
II. Title.
E185.97.M26A3   1988   977.1'00496073024 [B]   87-29845
ISBN 0-911704-48-5

Foreword to the
Bicentennial Edition

When Professor Allan Peskin prepared the first edition of *North Into Freedom* in 1966, he used an original printing of the John Malvin autobiography in the Western Reserve Historical Society Library as the basis for his work. That rare pamphlet was one part of a remarkable collection of hundreds of other books, photographs, and documents relating to the African-American experience then preserved in the Society's library collections.

In the three decades that have elapsed, *North Into Freedom* has been reprinted and enjoyed wide popularity, and the topic it represents--African American history--has grown to enjoy wide academic and popular appeal. In those same years, the Historical Society's collections relating to the history of the African-American experience in northeastern Ohio have grown a hundred fold. Its African American Archives stands now as one of the premiere programs of its kind. Today, the archives continues to seek and collect materials that will, like John Malvin's autobiography, inform generations about the lives of the ordinary and extraordinary people who have lived in northeastern Ohio.

The Western Reserve Historical Society is delighted to present this reprint of *North Into Freedom* in 1996, the Bicentennial of the founding of the City of Cleveland. It is particularly grateful to Werner D. Mueller for underwriting this effort. As with the other titles included in the Werner D. Mueller Reprint series, *North Into Freedom* helps the Western Reserve Historical Society accomplish its mission of preserving and providing direct access to the history and heritage of all of the people of northeast Ohio.

Richard L. Ehrlich
Executive Director

ACKNOWLEDGMENTS

Even a small book requires help from many hands. My interest in Cleveland Negro history was stimulated by a seminar with Dean Carl F. Wittke of Western Reserve University. It was Dean Wittke who suggested that I pursue Malvin's life further and now, ten years later, I am heeding his suggestion. Professor Harvey Wish, also of Western Reserve, encouraged me to carry the project through to completion, and the late Willis Thornton was generous with both encouragement and advice. I would like to express my thanks to Mr. Russell Davis for allowing me to examine an unpublished history of the Negro in Cleveland by Harry E. Davis. Cleveland State University gave me needed clerical assistance, and my wife, Barbara, patiently read proof and tried to instruct me in the mysteries of the comma and the semicolon. A special debt is due to the library of the Western Reserve Historical Society for allowing me to photocopy its volume of Malvin's *Autobiography*. I also appreciate the help I received from the Cleveland Public Library and the libraries of Western Reserve and Cleveland State Universities.

Contents

Introduction

i

John Malvin, whose autobiography is here reprinted, was a Negro freeman born in Virginia who emigrated north to Ohio in 1827. Malvin belonged to America's most forgotten of forgotten men. The free Negro before the Civil War was the orphan of American society, unwanted and ignored. "We know less of them than we know of the people of France and Italy," claimed one sympathizer.[1] On the eve of the Civil War over half a million free Negroes lived in the United States, roughly one-ninth of the total colored population. Their position in American society was an anomalous one: "They stand among us, yet not of us."[2] Nowhere, neither North nor South, were they welcomed.

In the South, the free Negro was hated and feared. By his very existence a free Negro was a living reproach to the slave system—a system which could justify itself only on the premise that the Negro was incapable of freedom. From the 1830's on, the free Negro in the South was increasingly repressed and degraded lest his successful example encourage the slaves to revolt. In many southern states his movements were regulated, his occupations restricted,

1

and his rights diminished until, by the late 1850's, some states of the Deep South were attempting to eliminate the problem entirely by expelling all free Negroes from their borders, forcing those who stayed behind to be sold into slavery.

If Negroes hoped to find a hospitable reception north of the Mason-Dixon Line, they were doomed to disappointment. Although the Northern states had rejected Negro slavery, they did not embrace the Negro. In most Northern states the Negro was regarded as a nuisance at best and at worst a menace to the prosperity of white working men. For a time many, North and South (including Abraham Lincoln), toyed with the notion of freeing the country from the awkward presence of the free Negro by encouraging him to emigrate to Liberia. Aside from the insurmountable practical obstacles involved, all colonization plans foundered against the resolute opposition of the Negro himself. Most Northern states adopted more practical and immediate measures to discourage Negroes from settling on their doorsteps, enacting rigid legal codes designed to harass the Negro and exclude him from participation in white society. In many Free States these legal codes were far more severe than the Black Codes or Black Laws that were drafted by the defeated Confederate states immediately after the Civil War, bodies of law that called down a storm of protest from the representatives of those very states that had only recently and reluctantly abandoned Black Codes of their own.

The status of the northern free Negro did not improve with the passage of time. On the contrary, in many states his position worsened. In the decade before the Civil War

2

many states stiffened their Black Codes and began to enforce forgotten old laws. This tendency was encouraged by the 1857 decision of the United States Supreme Court in the Dred Scott case, which characterized Negroes as "beings of an inferior order, and altogether unfit to associate with the white race, either in social or political relations; and so far inferior, that they had no rights which the white man was bound to respect." Only a year before the election of Lincoln it could be said that:

> In most of the Free States they are not allowed
> to vote, nor admitted into the public schools,
> are driven from places of public amusement
> and from the public conveyances, and are not
> permitted by social sentiment to engage in
> more than ten or twelve out of the three
> hundred and more occupations set down in the
> census for the white population.[3]

The most stringent anti-Negro legislation in the North was enacted in the states of the Old Northwest, in an area sometimes known as "The Valley of Democracy." In Illinois it was a misdemeanor for a Negro to enter the state to set up permanent residence. Such Negroes were to be fined and, if unable to pay the fine, could (theoretically) be sold into temporary slavery.[4] Indiana barred Negroes altogether by the state constitution of 1851, a constitution approved by a popular vote of more than five to one.[5]

ii

Ohio, the first midwestern state to be organized, set the pattern for the region. According to an early observer,

3

William Jay, a pioneer abolitionist and son of John Jay, "Prejudice against the Negro attains its rankest luxuriance, not in the swamps of Georgia, nor the sugar-fields of Louisiana but upon the prairies of Ohio."[6] Ohio's geographic position gave it an irresistible attraction to Southern Negroes, both slave and free: just across the river lay the Promised Land of Liberty. They were soon disillusioned, just as John Malvin was.

From its very earliest days Ohio took steps to ward off Negro immigration. Although the first constitution of Ohio prohibited slavery, it by no means encouraged Negro settlement. Despite the insignificant number of Negroes in Ohio at the time—only 337—the Negro question received careful consideration at the Constitutional Convention of 1802. At the Convention it was decided, in some cases by a very narrow margin, to deprive the Negro of the ballot, to exclude him from public office, and to prohibit him from testifying against white men in court.

In succeeding years the rights of Negroes in Ohio were restricted even further by that state's Black Laws. The first of these, passed in 1804, provided that no Negro could reside in Ohio without a court certificate declaring him to be a freeman and not an escaped slave. Negroes who entered a county had to register with the county clerk. If a white man hired a Negro without such a certificate, the employer could be fined, and if the Negro's owner put in an appearance the employer was required to pay fifty cents for each day the Negro had been employed.[7] In 1807 a more stringent set of regulations required all Negroes who entered the state to post a five-hundred-dollar bond "to pay for their support in case of want." Since few, if any,

4

Negro immigrants had that much money, the effect of this law, if enforced, would have been to cut off Negro immigration completely. Another section of this law put into statutory form the constitutional prohibition of Negro testimony in cases involving white men.[8] In 1803 Negroes were barred from the state militia, and in 1831 they were effectively excluded from juries by a law limiting jury service to those with the "qualifications of electors." Negroes were also excluded from state poorhouses, insane asylums, and other public institutions.

If the authors of these laws intended thereby to discourage Negroes from entering the state, the laws were unsuccessful. Negroes did not come to Ohio to serve on juries or in the militia, nor was a penniless Negro likely to be deterred by the prospect of forfeiting a five-hundred-dollar bond. The Black Laws served to harass those Negroes who were in Ohio, but they failed to discourage immigration. In any event, the force of these laws was greatly softened by lax administration. If they had been vigorously enforced virtually no Negroes could have entered Ohio, yet by 1849, the year of the repeal of the Black Laws, almost twenty-five thousand were living in the state. Nonetheless, even though some of the Black Laws were flouted, their very presence on the statute books served as a silent threat—and, on occasion, much more than that. In 1830 almost eighty Negroes were driven out of Portsmouth for failure to register and post bond, and in the preceding year, as Malvin relates, over a thousand Cincinnati Negroes had been compelled to leave for Canada in the wake of a revival of Black Law enforcement.

Some of the Black Laws were consistently enforced,

5

especially the law that prohibited Negro court testimony. Of all the Black Laws this was the most onerous, for without the protection of the courts no Ohio Negro could be secure in his life or property. Thieves could break into a Negro's home with impunity, as happened in Cincinnati in 1834. In this case, even though one of the thieves confessed, none of them could be convicted since the court had no proof, other than the inadmissible testimony of the victimized Negroes, that the property had been stolen. In a more extreme case, a public, daylight murder of a Negro by a white man went unpunished, since only Negroes were available as witnesses.[9]

In addition to all the legal restrictions embodied in the Black Laws, an unwritten code of segregation further confined the daily lives and opportunities of Ohio Negroes. Churches and theaters either barred Negroes entirely or else shunted them off to a separate gallery. No hotel or restaurant would serve a colored man in its dining room, generally insisting that he take his meals in the kitchen, though sometimes a colored servant might be allowed to eat with his master. Negroes were not allowed to ride a stagecoach if any white passenger objected. It was difficult for a Negro to find any job other than those menial tasks regarded as unfit for white men. When a Negro artisan was hired by a Cincinnati firm the white workers stalked off the job, declaring, "We won't work with a nigger," and remained on strike until the Negro was fired.[10]

In spite of the formidable obstacles, both legal and social, that faced the Negro in Ohio, Negroes, undaunted, persisted in coming to the state. Their numbers grew steadily, keeping pace with the white population. From

6

1800 to 1860 the proportion of Negroes in the Ohio population hovered around 1 per cent, indicating that the Negro community grew at the same pace and responded to the same trends as did the general population. This remarkable consistency also exposed the futility of the Black Laws, since their repeal was not followed by the feared influx of Negroes from other states.

Most of Ohio's Negroes came from the Border States where, like Malvin, they had been free men even before coming north. Although they came from rural areas, they tended to cluster in the cities, where the opportunities, such as they were, existed. Unlike his southern counterpart, the northern Negro was a city-dweller, living in urban slums for which his rural background ill-prepared him.

Some Ohio Negroes managed to escape the cities, and they advised their brethren to follow their example. A prosperous Negro agricultural colony in Mercer County asked those Negroes

> who live in towns and follow those precarious
> occupations for a livelihood, which prejudice has
> assigned to you, would you not be serving your
> country and your race to more purpose, if you
> were to leave your present residences and employ-
> ments, and go into the country and become a
> part of the bone and sinew of the land? . . . Our
> employment must be of that character that peo-
> ple can see how we obtain our livelihood, and
> that we are useful. What is it to the state when
> a waiter, or a bootblack, or a cook dies?[11]

The advice was well-meant but impractical. Few Ohio Negroes had either the capital or the skills needed for

7

success on the farm. Cincinnati, the most southern and by far the largest of Ohio's cities, held the greatest concentration of Negro population. By the Civil War over one out of every ten Ohio Negroes was living there. Cincinnati Negroes did not prosper. Their occupational and social status put them at the very bottom of the ladder. An informal survey conducted in 1845 revealed that there were 2,049 Negroes in Cincinnati, 364 of whom admitted they once were slaves. Of 1,103 adults, only 343 could read and write. Negroes owned slightly over $150,000 worth of property, an average of only $75 per person. Although there was a sprinkling of skilled workers in various trades—such as shoemakers, bricklayers, cabinet makers, and blacksmiths—the bulk of Cincinnati's Negro population held low-status, low-income jobs. The largest single category was that of common laborer, with 94. Rivermen followed, with 77. Washerwomen, with 64, constituted the next largest group, indicating that many families were held together by the labor of women. (Had domestic servants been included in the survey they might well have constituted the largest category.) Barbers and waiters, with 58 and 31 respectively, made up the next largest groups.[12]

In Cincinnati, then, Negroes were over-crowded, underpaid, and ill-treated. But in Cleveland, Malvin's home, where Negroes were few, their status was different. There they were able to win, after a time, a measure of dignity and civil acceptance scarcely matched anywhere in the nation.

iii

The first Negroes had come to the Cleveland region as

8

early as 1799, even before the area was officially open for settlement. Despite this early start, the Negro community grew slowly. Until the early 1830's Cleveland's Negroes constituted a tiny, unorganized band, scarcely noticed by the white population. This was hardly surprising. Cleveland itself was little more than a village. In 1831, the year of Malvin's arrival, Cleveland had only 1,100 inhabitants. A visitor from Rochester in that year, while admitting that the village presented "the pleasantest sight that you ever saw," was appalled at the high prices and low morals he found there. He noted that although the four churches barely struggled along with less than a half-dozen members each, "there are between fifteen and twenty grog-shops, and they all live."[13]

The Ohio Canal, which was responsible for the growth of Cleveland from a village to a city, was also responsible for the first influx of Negroes. Before the canal was built, Cleveland, though potentially a fine lakeport, could not tap the hinterland of downstate Ohio. The early settlers came from New England and upstate New York, following the lines of water transportation which ran from east to west. Since Negroes, by and large, came from the South, they tended to avoid the arduous overland route to Cleveland. The canal, which brought Malvin to Cleveland, changed all this. By 1834 there were enough Negroes in Cleveland to prompt the county officials to begin to comply with the law requiring that all incoming Negroes be registered by the clerk of courts.[14] Although the Negro population was now visible, it was far from sizeable. In 1844 there were still only 106 Negroes in Cleveland; in 1850, 224; in 1860, 779; and by 1870, when Cleveland had

9

become the fifteenth largest city in the nation, with over 92,000 inhabitants, only 1,293 of them were Negroes.

This slow, unspectacular growth helped shape the character of the Cleveland Negro community. Since the growth of the Negro population barely kept pace with the growth of the city, Negroes were easily absorbed into the community. There was, at first, some resistance, as Malvin discovered when he failed to find work as a carpenter because of his color. This resistance was due to the fears of white workingmen that Negro competition might depress their own status. This hostility was expressed at a mass meeting called to support the Black Laws. The meeting condemned Negro migration, "whereby our state has become the common receptacle of a class of beings disqualified by nature from any society but their own,—unaquainted with or disregarding the ordinary means of procuring an honest living, so that they are unavoidably driven to seek their associates among the most degraded and vicious of the white population thereby fearfully augmenting that already too numerous class by whom our property is daily plundered and our lives jeopardized."[15]

Even at the time, however, this was a minority view, and these fears soon faded as public opinion moved rapidly in the direction of a greater degree of sympathy for Cleveland's Negro population. The success of the anti-slavery movement on the Western Reserve in the 1840's and 1850's did much to dispel the early prejudice. If Clevelanders were concerned over the plight of the southern slave, they could not, in all consistency, spurn him if he took their advice, escaped from his bondage, and came to dwell among them.

10

Abolitionism may have helped create a favorable social climate, but Cleveland Negroes were not merely the beneficiaries of politically inspired good will. They *earned* the respect of the white community by the manner in which they took advantage of the opportunities open to them. Within a decade of Malvin's arrival, Cleveland could boast of a sprinkling of successful Negro artisans, tradesmen, and small entrepreneurs who gave their colored community a middle-class flavor unmatched anywhere in the country. "They are," said the Cleveland *Herald*, with evident pride, "industrious, peaceable, intelligent and ambitious of improvement."[16] Twenty years later, James Freeman Clarke, the Boston abolitionist, was delighted to find in Cleveland an exception to the general rule of Negro degradation. "The feeling toward them in Cleveland, and throughout the Western Reserve," he reported in 1859, "is very kind, and there they do better than in most places. There you find them master carpenters, master painters, shopkeepers, and growing rich every year."[17]

The observation was exaggerated. No Cleveland Negroes were rich, and many lived in brutal poverty. There were, in fact, two Negro communities in Cleveland. One was composed of reasonably well-off, respectable artisans and tradesmen who attended meetings, formed clubs, and signed petitions. The other was made up of nameless drifters, huddled in Negro shanties clustered by the riverfront, who made no mark on the community except when they brawled, drank, or drowned in the river.[18]

There were, however, enough successful examples of Negro thrift and enterprise in Cleveland to counterbalance in the public mind the unfavorable image created by the

11

shiftless minority. In 1845, for example, it was estimated that 20 of the city's 160 Negroes owned real estate. With their families, these 20 men accounted for 56 people, one-third of Cleveland's Negro population. Almost half of these men had once been slaves, yet now they owned a total of $35,000 in property and followed a number of respectable occupations requiring special skills. They numbered among them carpenters, masons, blacksmiths, and canal-boat captains.[19]

This occupational versatility was one of the hallmarks of the Cleveland Negro community. In contrast to Cincinnati, where Negroes were virtually confined to menial trades, Cleveland Negroes enjoyed rather wide opportunities. A roll call of prominent Cleveland Negroes before the Civil War indicates the extent of these opportunities. Freeman Morris was a well-patronized tailor. Mr. Swing manufactured a popular coffee pot which he had invented, and George Peake made and sold his patented hand mill. Alfred Greenbrier bred horses on his farm off Bridge Avenue, on the near West Side. George Vosburgh worked for the railroad, but his principal income came from property, which he rented to white as well as Negro tenants. A number of Cleveland Negroes were shopkeepers, with grocery and provision stores. Some even followed the professions. Mrs. Osborne Stanley taught in the Cleveland public schools, to classes of white as well as Negro children. William Howard Day was a librarian and newspaperman, and Dr. R. B. Leach was a physician with a degree from Cleveland's own Homeopathic College. And then, of course, there was Malvin, a jack-of-all-trades.

Not all Cleveland Negroes were so fortunate or enterprising. The city had its share of colored waiters, porters, draymen, and barbers. Some of these men, however, were fairly well-to-do, especially the barbers. Before the Italian immigration of the early twentieth century, Negroes virtually monopolized the barber trade in Cleveland, and the more successful, such as John Brown and John L. Watson, became well-known and respected Negro spokesmen. A few years later, Mark Hanna's barber, George A. Myers, became a local power in the Republican Party, dispensing sage advice to Hanna along with haircuts.[20]

By the Civil War, then, many Cleveland Negroes had managed to attain a secure economic position. They were equally fortunate in their relations with the white community, enjoying what was for the time an exceptional freedom from prejudice and discrimination. The two achievements were not unrelated. James Freeman Clarke was aware of the close correlation between economic and social status. "Colored people ought to make money," he suggested. "A colored man who makes $1000 does more to put down prejudice than if he made 1000 moderately good speeches against prejudice, or wrote 1000 pretty fair articles against it."[21]

iv

The more blatant forms of prejudice, so common in most parts of the state, were virtually unknown in Cleveland after 1850. As one newspaper remarked with pride, "colored children attend all our public schools, and colored people are permitted to attend all public lectures and public affairs where the fashion and culture of the city con-

13

gregate, and nobody is offended."[22] Every now and then a southern visitor would return home with stories of eating in a supposedly respectable Cleveland restaurant and finding that "two buck Negroes deliberately seated themselves opposite,"[23] but most of the natives didn't seem to mind. Those who did were pointedly reminded that even before the Civil War Cleveland could boast of "colored citizens" (and Malvin was specifically included by name) who were "old, intelligent, industrious and respectable citizens, who own property, pay taxes, vote at elections, educate their children in public schools, and contribute to build up the institutions and to the advancement of the prosperity of the city. . . ."[24]

Of no city in the nation outside of New England could such a claim have been made. By the turn of the century Cleveland was being touted as "The Negroes' Paradise," a city where the Negro enjoyed "almost complete equality with the white man." The people of Cleveland, it was asserted, "have come near to furnishing to the world at large an ideal condition of affairs between the white and colored races."[25]

This evaluation was over-optimistic. Even in Malvin's day, before the flush of abolitionist idealism had faded, there were signs of racial inequality in Cleveland. The Academy of Music, Cleveland's most fashionable theater, refused to seat Negroes anywhere but in the balcony.[26] Segregation on streetcars lingered until the Civil War was almost over.[27] Colored barbers found that their white customers objected to being clipped with the same shears that cut Negro hair.[28] These vestiges of segregation were irritating but were

14

no more than pinpricks. A more serious matter was the inequitable treatment that was accorded Negroes in Cleveland courts. Even after the repeal of the Black Laws, Negro lawbreakers were generally sentenced more severely than their white counterparts, and crimes against Negroes were often punished more lightly than equivalent crimes against white men. In 1849, for example, two white men were sentenced to only two and four years in the penitentiary for a brutal and unprovoked murder of a Negro. That same day the court sentenced a burglar to three years, and a white citizen who stabbed another white man with *intent* to kill received a five-year term.[29] When Negroes began to serve on juries, in the 1870's, this disparity began to lessen. Curiously enough, though, the early juries on which Negroes served were all-colored juries, convened for cases in which a Negro was the defendant, indicating the persistence of a double standard of justice.[30]

Social discrimination was even more persistent than legal discrimination. Negroes and whites inhabited different worlds, seldom visiting each other's homes or meeting together for any purely social occasion. Even so sympathetic a journal as the Cleveland *Herald* was shocked by a report that Oberlin College had sponsored a dinner attended jointly by white and colored men and women.[31] Enemies of the Negro, such as the then notoriously negrophobic *Plain Dealer*, saw the specter of intermarriage in such social mingling, warning that social equality would "amalgamate the races and make this a government of minks and monkeys."[32]

Even though there were these limits to Cleveland's capacity for racial tolerance, that capacity was nonethe-

15

less remarkable. How did Cleveland develop such striking racial harmony? One factor seems to have been the relatively small number of Negroes in the city. In many places racial tolerance was apparently inversely proportional to the number of Negroes the community found it necessary to tolerate. Neighboring Geauga County, for example, had won the reputation of being the most dedicated abolitionist region in the nation by 1850, a year when the census-taker could find only seven Negroes in the entire county.

Another factor working to elevate the status of the Cleveland Negro was the abolition movement, which on the Western Reserve had almost the force of a crusade. But this factor worked both ways. It is conceivable that abolitionism owed no small part of its appeal in Cleveland to the example set by the local Negroes, an example that seemed to demonstrate that the Negro could survive and even flourish in freedom.

There was yet another factor, perhaps the most important of all, and it is on this point that Malvin's memoir is especially illuminating. In Cleveland, unlike many other cities, Negroes themselves were active champions of their cause rather than hopeful, passive recipients of the white man's benevolence. The civil rights movement in Cleveland was unique in that it was begun by Negroes, and Malvin can be considered its founder. When he refused to be segregated in a rear pew of the First Baptist Church, Malvin set a pattern that would be followed for the next fifty years or more. If a Negro could pray next to a white man, it was not unreasonable for that Negro to expect that they could work together, live side by side, and send their children to the same school. Malvin's integration of the churches raised the expectations of Cleveland Negroes and by accustoming them to equality in one sphere of activity led them to demand it in others.

To secure their rights, Cleveland Negroes, sparked by Malvin among others, learned how to organize and act as a coherent interest group. They were active in the movement to repeal the Black Laws and eagerly agitated to correct other grievances. The insistence with which they presented their demands belied the condescending estimate of those who liked to picture the Negro as a simple, childlike creature, content "to pass gaily down the stream of time, enjoying the sunshine of an almost perpetual infancy."[33] On the contrary, Cleveland Negroes were a decidedly militant lot, ready to hold a meeting, call a convention, circulate a petition, or pressure a legislator at the slightest provocation.

In addition to defense organizations (usually temporary, *ad hoc* groups), Cleveland Negroes created a host of other groups. The variety and scope of their activities were impressive in view of the small size of the local Negro community. Self-help and educational societies flourished, especially in the years before the repeal of the Black Laws and the establishment of adequate public schools for Negroes. The Young Men's Union Society of 1839 was designed to promote reading and debating, "in order that we may become good and virtuous citizens and not be a disgrace to our country by our ignorance."[34] Fraternal orders flourished, with the Masons organizing in 1855 and the Odd Fellows three years later. A Negro militia company was a colorful attraction in local parades from 1858

17

on and was an indispensable feature of the festivities at the annual celebration of West Indian emancipation on August 3, a day commemorated with parades, prayer meetings, picnics, brass bands, and orations, as a sort of Negro Fourth of July.

Cultural activities were not neglected. In addition to musical groups, such as bands and singing societies, Cleveland Negroes organized lecture series and theatrical events. In 1853 they established their own theatrical company, and a local playwright, James B. Smith, ground out crude but topical melodramas for the colored troupe to perform.[35]

A further indication of the exceptional degree of group consciousness existing among Cleveland Negroes was the fact that they had, for a time, their own newspaper: a short-lived journal begun in 1853 and called *The Aliened American.* This was one of the first Negro papers in the nation and was, at the time, the only one west of New York state. The enterprise was a failure, but that it should have been attempted at all by such a small Negro community was significant.

In all this flurry of organizational activity, one group was inconspicuous. In most communities, Negro social life was dominated by the church. In Cleveland, however, the Negro church lacked both influence and prestige. After Malvin had persuaded the Baptists to admit Negroes on equal terms, the other churches followed suit. For Malvin, this was a triumph; but for the Negro churches it was a disaster. Faced with competition from integrated, well-established congregations, the all-Negro churches were compelled to struggle along with low membership and meager funds. Although the first Negro church, St. John's African Methodist Episcopal, was founded as early as 1830, it was not able to afford a permanent home for another eighteen years. The leaders of the Cleveland Negro community shunned the segregated churches whose ranks were filled, by and large, with former slaves who felt ill at ease in the decorous gentility of the white man's church and preferred the familiar, emotional style of the fundamentalist religion as it was practiced on the plantation. Three out of the five original trustees of St. John's A.M.E. church could not even write their names.[36] Clearly, their church could not command the loyalties of the educated aspirants to the middle-class who constituted the bulk of Cleveland's Negro community. Consequently, Cleveland Negroes turned to other organizations to fill the social gap left by the church.

As an indirect and unexpected result of Malvin's integration of the churches, Cleveland Negroes became a community of organizers and joiners. Of all their number, none was a more assiduous joiner than Malvin himself. For almost half a century no meeting of Cleveland Negroes seemed official unless Malvin were somewhere on the rostrum. From the very early days when he organized the first Negro school committee and planned the first convention until the end of his long, busy life, Malvin was a leading spirit among Cleveland Negroes. He was not always the most influential leader, but he was certainly a ubiquitous one. His autobiography gives an indication of some of his projects, but only by leafing through the yellowed pages of Cleveland's newspapers can one get a glimpse of the full range of his activities. Now he is seen speaking against the hated Black Laws; later, organizing a celebration for their repeal. In 1850 he shares the platform with Frederick Douglass to commemorate West Indian emancipation; not long after that, he raises money to redeem a family from slavery, and then is off on a lecture tour for the Ohio Anti-Slavery Society. During the war he addresses meetings and drafts resolutions to persuade the government to channel the wartime idealism into a crusade for equal rights. After the war he is in demand as a Republican campaign speaker, advocating Radical Reconstruction, praising the passage of the Fifteenth Amendment, and mourning the passing of Thaddeus Stevens.

By the 1870's Malvin had become a well-known and even beloved Cleveland figure—"Father John." Early in 1877 his friends gave a testimonial dinner to honor a man "who has labored hard for the elevation of the colored race."[37] Possibly the idea of writing his memoirs was stimulated by this dinner. In any event, his *Autobiography* appeared in 1879, a modest booklet of forty-two pages jobprinted by the Cleveland *Leader*.

The book was written from an old man's memory and, as Malvin warns the reader in the preface, some of his dates are inaccurate (these have been corrected, when possible, in the footnotes of the present edition). Other errors of detail crept in, as for example, "Dominick" for Harmon Blennerhasset, and certain recollections seem to be exaggerated, such as the three-hundred-mile hike from Virginia to Ohio, which surely must have taken him more than six days. But, by and large, when Malvin spoke of events he had witnessed personally, his memory was remarkably reliable, even though the interpretations he sometimes placed on these events were not always profound or convincing. His implications against Hiram V. Willson, to cite one example, seem inconsistent with Willson's subsequent career and should not be accepted without further evidence.

Aside from these few cautions, no elaborate commentary or analysis seems necessary. Malvin's narrative speaks for itself. It is here reproduced in its original form, without alteration of spelling or punctuation. The book mirrors the man: direct, unadorned, dignified, and optimistic.

Malvin recorded his memoirs none too soon. The year after they were published, when he was 85 years old according to his reckoning, he died, on September 29, 1880, and was buried in Erie Cemetery. His death and funeral were regarded as newsworthy events, and the *Leader* took the unusual step of printing a column-long obituary which chronicled "The Eventful Career and Noble Work of a Worthy Man Whose Thoughts Were of his People." Through editorial thrift (or laziness) the obituary was lifted, without acknowledgement, from Malvin's book. "After an eventful life of hardships and toil, spent in the good and advancement of his kind," the eulogy concluded, "John Malvin passed away to that land where the black and the white man are surely on an equality."[38]

To this pious hope, Malvin surely would have said, "Amen." Yet he also looked for equality in this world. His goal was never completely achieved, but he remained confident throughout his life because of the progress he had seen and had, in fact, helped to create.

Fortunately for Malvin's optimism, he did not live to

see his faith in God, Progress, and the Republican Party challenged by the deterioration in race relations that set in with the twentieth century. He could die echoing the prayer of Julia Foote, the former slave turned evangelist: "I shall praise God through all eternity for sending me to Cleveland."[39] In the code of the Underground Railroad, Cleveland was "Hope." For Malvin, and for hundreds of other Negroes, that hope was fulfilled. Indeed, his life and his work did much to keep that hope alive.

ALLAN PESKIN

Cleveland, Ohio
May 1, 1966

NOTES TO THE INTRODUCTION

[1] Rev. James Freeman Clarke, *Present Condition of the Free People of Color of the United States* (New York, 1859), p. 3.

[2] *Ibid.*

[3] *Ibid.*

[4] Illinois Public Laws (1853), in Franklin Johnson, *The Development of State Legislation Concerning the Free Negro* (New York, 1918), p. 96.

[5] Indiana Constitution of 1851, Art. XIII, in Johnson, *Development of State Legislation,* p. 99.

[6] Frank U. Quillin, *The Color Line in Ohio: A History of Race Prejudice in a Typical Northern State* (Ann Arbor, 1913), p. 45.

[7] Acts of Ohio (1803-1804), in Johnson, *Development of State Legislation,* p. 161.

[8] Laws of Ohio (1806-1807), in Johnson, *Development of State Legislation,* p. 161.

[9] Ohio Anti-Slavery Society, *Report on the Condition of the People of Color in the State of Ohio* (Boston, 1836), p. 3.

[10] *Ibid.*

[11] *Daily Herald* (Cleveland), August 26, 1843.

[12] *Ibid.*, November 1, 1845.

[13] Cited in James Henry Kennedy, *A History of the City of Cleveland; Its Settlement, Rise and Progress* (Cleveland, 1896), pp. 237-38. By 1857 Cleveland had grown to almost fifty thousand, but the saloons (154 according to the City Directory) still outnumbered the churches by a substantial margin.

[14] *Ibid.*, pp. 260-61. In 1896 Kennedy claimed to have seen this registration book in the "dusty files of the clerk of courts." Since then the book has been lost somewhere in the vast county archives. Hopefully, it will be rediscovered someday, for no full history of Cleveland's Negroes can be written without the information it must contain.

[15] *Daily Herald* (Cleveland), September 17, 1841.

[16] *Herald and Gazette* (Cleveland), March 28, 1839.

[17] Clarke, *Present Condition*, p. 23.

[18] This floating population was overwhelmingly masculine, which may account for a curious statistical anomaly. In 1860, there were 105.9 Negro men for every 100 Negro women in Cleveland. This ratio was higher than the ratio anywhere else in the country except for the frontier settlements of California, and it contrasts with Cincinnati's ratio of 96.4 and the nearly normal sex ratio of 101.2 for Ohio Negroes as a whole. See Wilbur Zelinsky, "The Population Geography of the Free Negro in *Ante-Bellum* America," *Population Studies*, III (1949-50), p. 400.

[19] *Daily Herald* (Cleveland), November 5, 1845.

[20] See John A. Garraty (ed.), *The Barber and the Historian: The Correspondence of George A. Myers and James Ford Rhodes, 1910-1923* (Columbus, 1956).

[21] Clarke, *Present Condition*, p. 26.

23

[22] *Leader* (Cleveland), March 7, 1865.

[23] *Ibid.*, May 6, 1865.

[24] *Ibid.*, February 8, 1858.

[25] Quillin, *The Color Line*, 154, 156.

[26] See, for example, the standing ad of the Academy of Music, *Leader* (Cleveland), January 3, 1866.

[27] *Ibid.*, July 2, 1864.

[28] *Ibid.*, February 22, 1865.

[29] *Daily True Democrat* (Cleveland), October 22-29, 1849.

[30] *Leader* (Cleveland), August 8, 1871.

[31] *Daily Herald* (Cleveland), August 8, 1842.

[32] Cited in *Leader* (Cleveland), August 1, 1857.

[33] Ohio General Assembly, *Report of a Select Committee Proposing to Repeal All Laws Creating Distinctions on Account of Color, Commonly Called the Black Laws. Report of the Minority* (In House, January 18, 1845), p. 9.

[34] *Herald and Gazette* (Cleveland), February 5, 1839.

[35] *Plain Dealer* (Cleveland), May 18, 1853; June 26, 1860.

[36] William Ganson Rose, *Cleveland: The Making of a City* (Cleveland and New York, 1950), p. 211.

[37] *Leader* (Cleveland), December 21, 1876.

[38] *Ibid.*, August 2, 1880.

[39] Julia A. J. Foote, *A Brand Plucked From the Fire: An Autobiographical Sketch* (Cleveland, 1879), p. 110.

AUTOBIOGRAPHY
of
JOHN MALVIN

A Narrative,

Containing an Authentic Account of His Fifty Years'
Struggle In the State of Ohio in Behalf of the Ameri-
can Slave, And The Equal Rights of All Men
Before the Law Without Reference to Race
or Color; Forty-Seven Years Of Said
Time Being Expended in the
City of Cleveland.

PREFACE

Many of my friends of this city desiring me to give to the public the history of my life, and the details and incidents connected therewith, I hesitated for a long time to make the undertaking, but from their continual solicitations, I at last concluded to write a narrative, which, strictly speaking, is no history of my life, but an enumeration of the principal events which have occurred, and with which I have been personally connected. Not having a record to guide me, I have been obliged to rely entirely on my memory. It is very possible, therefore, that there may be some slight errors as to dates and matters of minor importance, but as to the events themselves, I can safely assure my friends that they are related substantially as they occurred.

Chapter One

I WAS BORN IN Prince William County, Virginia, in the year 1795, in a little town known by the name of Dumfries.[1] My mother, whose name was Dalcus Malvin, was a free woman, but my father was a slave belonging to a man named Henderson. In my seventh year I was bound out to this Henderson as an apprentice. Henderson also lived in Dumfries, owned several farms in Wood County, W. Va.,[2] and was a large slave owner. He had a clerk named John Griffith, who was an unmarried man, and whose business it was to keep the accounts of the several farms, and I was assigned by Mr. Henderson to wait upon this clerk. I attended him personally, blacked his boots, took care of his horse, and so on, and when through

---

[1] Dumfries is on the Potomac estuary, about twenty-five miles south of the District of Columbia.

[2] Until 1863, of course, there was no such state as West Virginia. Wood County (created in 1798) was part of Virginia when Malvin was a boy.

with these avocations, at times, I would go out into the field and work with the other hands. At dinner time my duty was to go to the house and prepare the table. After dinner I would return again to the field. Such was my daily employment.

I was kept regularly at this employment for nearly four years, when, in the year 1807, the people of Wood County were greatly agitated and aroused by the discovery of a plotted rebellion, which had been fomented by Dominick Blennerhassett[3] and Aaron Burr, who had their head-quarters at Blennerhassett Island, on the Ohio River, three miles below the mouth of the Little Kanawha. I was at that time removed from my present situation to one of the farms in that vicinity, situated on what is known as Cow Creek, and remained there until the breaking out of the war of 1812. Griffith had preceded me to this farm, and when I arrived there I was kept at substantially the same occupation. During this period I had a fair opportunity of witnessing the miseries of slavery. Though I was an apprentice, I was treated little better than a slave myself. For my clothing, I was supplied every year with one pair of shoes, two pairs of tow linen pantaloons, one pair of negro cotton pantaloons, and a negro cotton round jacket. My food consisted of one peck of corn meal a week. Sometimes I re-

---

[3] Harmon (not Dominick) Blennerhasset was the wealthy Irish-born owner of Blennerhasset Island on the Ohio River. In 1806 (not 1807) he was implicated in Aaron Burr's alleged conspiracy, although neither Burr's intentions nor Blennerhasset's role have ever been satisfactorily explained.

ceived a supply of salt, but they were very sparing of that luxury, and I was compelled most of the time to go without it. I was obliged to resort to other means to obtain food.

The luxury which I observed among the neighboring slave-owners, and the style of living of my master, stimulated my appetite for some of the good things of this world, and being of an adventurous spirit, like most other boys, I concluded to avail myself of any means that would enable me to procure something more substantial than corn meal. There was another boy on the farm who was a little older than myself, and who roomed with me in the same cabin. Whenever we felt a desire for meat we would provide ourselves with clubs, and in the night time visit the hog beds. The hogs were allowed to run at large in the woods, and when we would find a sow with her pigs, we would drive her up and make a selection of one of the pigs, and by good use of our clubs secure the fruit of our adventure. We would then take the pig to our cabin, make a hot fire, and, instead of scalding, we would singe the hair off from the pig. Then we would dress and roast the pig to our fancy, which, with our corn bread, made us a meal which we relished all the more by reason of the risk and danger we ran in obtaining it. When we wanted a change in our diet we would go out among the cows and get some milk. In our first adventure of this kind I procured a jug; I inserted the teat into the mouth of the jug and was about to proceed milking, when the cow made a sudden movement with one of her hind legs and struck me on the thigh. I fell over and lay until the pain subsided, when I got up and found

31

another cow more docile than the first, and succeeded in getting the jug filled. Roast pig was well enough in its way, but we sometimes wanted a change of meat, and then we would go out among the sheep and catch a lamb, and unbutton its collar (cut its throat).

One night I had retired as usual, to sleep, but before retiring I had placed a pot of water over the fire place, in which I had put my shirt to boil. When I woke up I found to my dismay that the pot was glowing red, and that all the water had boiled out. At the bottom of the pot was a hand full of ashes, being all that remained of my shirt. This was the only shirt I had, and when I notified the clerk of my mishap, in order to recompense me for my loss, he gave me a severe flogging, and through the whole winter I was obliged to go without a shirt on my back and no covering but my jacket.

On the breaking out of the war of 1812 I attempted to run away, and for that purpose I followed a body of soldiers. I attempted to get aboard one of their boats on the Ohio River, but not succeeding, I was compelled to return to my station, and I never was missed, nor was the fact of my leaving ever discovered.

On another occasion I was taken by this clerk Griffith, my wrists were tied crosswise together, and my hands were then brought down and tied to my ankles; my shirt was taken off, and in that condition I was compelled to lie on the ground, and he began flogging me. He whipped me on one side till the flesh was all raw and bleeding; then he rolled me over like a log and whipped me on the other side in the same manner. When I was untied I put on my shirt. So severely was my flesh lacerated that my shirt stuck to my back, and I was unable to get it off without the assistance of an old lady who lived on the farm, who applied grease to it. I had committed no crime or offense that justified any such treatment. He had ordered me to chop some logs, so that they could be rolled together to be burned. His brother was to attend to the burning of the logs, and I had chopped them and went away. The logs had been rolled together and a fire started, but by some accident the fire reached the fence and burnt five or six of the panels. As soon as I heard of this I ran to the fence and stopped the fire from spreading, and sat there until 12 o'clock at night to watch and keep the cattle from going through into the corn. The clerk then came home and finding things in this condition, he stripped and whipped me in the manner I have stated. I resolved at that time that if ever I should grow older and stronger I would kill him, but I never got an opportunity to be revenged upon him, as in 1813 Mr. Henderson died, and I was at liberty again, and returned to my parents in East Virginia, and never saw the clerk afterwards.

My father was a carpenter by trade, and I began to work with him at his bench until I had learned the trade. During the time I was working with my father I became possessed of a desire to learn to read. When I would see people read a newspaper or book, I felt great delight in what seemed to me to be *pretty talking,* as I considered it. When I heard any one read, my curiosity would be excited, and

33

I would listen attentively to the matter read, and I at last concluded that I should like to *talk pretty* too, like the white people. An excellent opportunity was afforded me. I knew an old slave who was past labor, and who lived in a cabin three miles from where I did, and who by some means had learned to read. He could read the Bible quite readily, and he consented to teach me to read and spell. We obtained light to read by means of pine knots, which I would go out and find in the dark by feeling with my feet. I would carry them to the old man's cabin and put them in the fire-place. We did not dare to talk loud, lest we should be overheard, and had to confine ourselves to whispers. Such were the means and circumstances under which I learned to read and spell. After I had learned to read I began to attend several religious meetings, and became so wrought up with religious fervor that I concluded to preach the gospel. I joined the Baptist Church, and, though I had no education, I applied to the church of which I was a member, for a license to preach. That not being permissible under the laws of Virginia, by reason of my color, the church refused to give me a license, but gave me a verbal permission to preach the gospel.

I began preaching among the slaves, and even solemnized marriages[4] by permission from the owners. While preaching, I continued to live with my parents, and re-

---

[4] Strictly speaking, marriage between slaves had no legal force. Sometimes, however, the owner would permit a mock ceremony for the sake of domestic harmony and sometimes just as an excuse for a celebration.

mained with them until 1827, during which time I availed myself of every opportunity I could get, to read, whenever I could obtain a paper or book. Nothing eventful occurred to me, however, during this period, until I left my home, as I shall relate in the following chapter.

Chapter Two

I N T H E Y E A R 1827, a spirit of adventure, natural to
most young men, took possession of me, and I concluded to leave Virginia and go to Ohio. No colored man
was permitted to travel through Virginia without produc-
ing evidences in some way of his freedom. I had a short time
prior to my departure, applied for and obtained freedom
papers, to which was affixed the signature of the Clerk of
the County, and the seal of the Court.

I affectionately took leave of my parents, with nothing
but my clothes that were on my back, and an extra shirt,
and started a foot on my journey, by way of what was called
the Winchester Road. The first village I came to after crossing Cedar Run, was Brentsville; the second was Hay Market, passing the Bull Run Mountain at what was called
the Thoroughfare Gap; then pursuing my course until I
came to Oak Hill, the residence of Chief Justice Marshall;
then crossing the Blue Ridge Mountain at Ashly's Gap,
then down along the Shenandoah River, crossing that at

Berry's Ferry, leaving Millwood and Whitepost to the left; thence to Winchester, Frederick County; thence crossing the south branch of the Potomac, near Rumley's and so on to Cheat River and Patterson Creek. At Rumley I stopped at a magistrates [*sic*] office and produced the necessary papers of my freedom, and was permitted to proceed. That was the only magistrate I called on during my journey. Shortly after leaving Rumley, I was met by two men, one of whom had a dog and rifle. They asked me who I was, and demanded proof. I showed them my papers, and they let me pass.

I forded all the streams mentioned, and then came to Clarksburg, the metropolis of Harrison County, thence to the Dry Ridge in Wood County, and from thence to the Ohio River, to the farm where I had formerly lived on Cow Creek; crossing Cow Creek, Calf Creek and Bull Creek and so on down the river, until I came opposite Marietta, and there I crossed by ferry. The boy who was rowing me over the river, had got to the middle of the stream, when he was discovered by his employer, who, seeing that I was a colored man, ordered the boy to row me back. He then asked me some questions, and I presented my freedom papers, and, after examining them he allowed the boy to row me across. I walked a distance of 300 miles, from Prince William County to Marietta, Ohio, in the short space of six days.

At Marietta, I got aboard of a flat boat on the Ohio River, and worked my passage to Cincinnati, which was then a growing town. I thought upon coming to a free State like Ohio, that I would find every door thrown open to receive me, but from the treatment I received by the people generally, I found it little better than in Virginia.[1]

I had not been long in Cincinnati, before I became acquainted with many of the colored people there residing, and it was there I first began to interest myself in the condition of my race. My attention had been called to a statute of Ohio, in which I read substantially these words: "That no negro or mulatto should be permitted to emigrate to this State, or settle, or acquire a domicile, without first entering into bonds of $500, with approved security, conditioned that he would never become a town charge, and that he would keep the peace." I read on a little further: "That no negro or mulatto shall testify in a Court of Justice or Record, where a party in a cause there pending was white. No negro or mulatto child shall enter into any of the public schools of this State, or receive the benefit of the school fund. No negro or mulatto shall be permitted to

---

[1] Another refugee who escaped into Ohio from slavery expressed his disappointment in verse:
Ohio's not the place for me:
For I was much surprised
So many of her sons to see
In garments of disguise.
Her name has gone throughout the world,
Free Labor—Soil—and men—
But slaves had better far be hurled
Into the lion's den.
Farewell, Ohio!
I cannot stop in thee.
I'll travel on to Canada,
Where colored men are free.

enter any of the institutions of this State, viz: a lunatic asylum, deaf and dumb asylum, nor even the poor house."

Thus I found every door closed against the colored man in a free State, excepting the jails and penitentiaries, the doors of which were thrown wide open to receive him.[2] I was for some time uncertain whether to remain in Ohio, or to return to Virginia, but at length concluded to remain in Ohio for a time, not knowing what to do. I succeeded in calling together a meeting of the colored men of Cincinnati, and, on consultation, things did not look very encouraging. I suggested to the meeting the propriety of appointing a committee to go to some country with power to make arrangements for the purchase of some place to live free from the trammels of unsocial and unequal laws.

None but those who have experienced the misery of servitude, or the pangs which result from the consciousness of being despised as a caste, from being shut out from the benefit of enjoying the pure atmosphere of heaven in common with all mankind, and not only being personally despised, but not even having the protection of the laws themselves, can fully appreciate the patriotic ardor which animated that little assembly. That we should find a home that we could consider wholly our own, where we could all be on an equal social footing, warmed us up to an un-

---

[2] In 1850, for example, out of every ten thousand whites in Ohio, 1.9 were prisoners in the state penitentiary, while out of every ten thousand Negroes, 17.4 were imprisoned there. In the Free States as a whole, two out of every ten thousand whites and twenty-eight out of every ten thousand Negroes were in prison.

40

usual degree of enthusiasm. A committee consisting of James King, Henry Archer and Israel Lewis, was appointed for that purpose. The committee went to Canada, and entered into negotiations with a Canadian Land Company, for 30,000 acres of land, located on the Sabel River, to form a colony. The colony was soon afterwards formed, and took the name of Wilberforce, after the great anti-slavery champion.[3]

During the time that the committee was absent, I called

---

[3] The Canadian colonization venture was not, as Malvin suggests, begun on his initiative but was made necessary by the action of the Trustees of Cincinnati, who threatened, in 1829, to begin rigid enforcement of the long-dormant Black Laws. Since nearly all of the approximately 2,250 Cincinnati Negroes lived in daily violation of these laws, their position threatened to become untenable, as they would no longer be able to find any employment were the laws enforced. Looking elsewhere for a possible haven, they formed a Colonization Society, headed by J. C. Brown. Malvin's role, if any, in these activities is unclear, but he does not seem to have been as prominent as his later recollection suggests.

The colony at Wilberforce was a sad failure. At first the Canadian government welcomed the scheme, and Israel Lewis made plans to buy an entire township (Biddulph) north of London, Ontario, for $600,000. In the meantime, however, Cincinnati had second thoughts and quietly shelved the projected Black Law enforcement, thus removing the chief incentive for emigration. Only 460 Negroes left for Canada, and of these only half a dozen families settled in the area set aside for purchase. They were soon joined by about fifteen Boston families, and in 1831 the small colony took the name Wilberforce, in honor of the British Methodist Bishop who led the successful struggle for West Indian slave emancipation. The region was wild, forbid-

41

a meeting of the colored men of Cincinnati, for the purpose of petitioning the Legislature for the repeal of those obnoxious black laws. We drew up a petition to which we obtained numerous signatures, and among others, those of Nicholas Longworth,[4] Wykoff Piatt[5] and John Klingman.

---

ding country, with only one stream, the Oxsable (not Sable) River, which ran dry each summer.

Inhospitable terrain, poor leadership, and shortage of funds doomed the project from the start. Only seventeen hundred acres were purchased, and in 1852 only twenty families could be found there. The population never exceeded seventy, and by the 1880's Wilberforce had virtually disappeared.

Israel Lewis contributed to the failure. A former slave who had escaped to Cincinnati in the grand manner, pursued by bloodhounds, Lewis was a man of considerable native ability whose personal magnetism exceeded his honesty. Charged with collecting funds for the project, he pocketed the money he collected and so alienated the Canadian land company that it refused to sell further land to any Negro. (See Fred Landon, "The History of the Wilberforce Refugee Colony in Middlesex County," *Transactions of the London and Middlesex Historical Society*, Part IX [1918], pp. 30-44.)

[4] Born in New Jersey in 1772 of a prominent family, Nicholas Longworth settled in Cincinnati in 1803 to practice as a lawyer. His willingness to accept land as payment for legal fees enabled him to become one of the richest men in Cincinnati, if not the entire nation. Retiring from the bar and land speculation, he turned to his hobby of horticulture, becoming a specialist in grape cultivation and an expert on the sex habits of the strawberry. Eccentric in dress and manner, Longworth was also unusual in his charitable behavior, preferring to give in secret. Anti-slavery by belief but not an abolitionist, he was a special benefactor to the Negro, purchasing runaway slaves and building Negro schools and orphan asylums. He died in 1863.

This petition, after it had been put in circulation, raised a great deal of comment. We saw published in one of the daily papers of Cincinnati, the following notice from members of one of the colored churches:[6]

"We, the undersigned, members of the Methodist Episcopal Church, 200 in number, do certify that we form no part of that indefinite number that are asking a change in the laws of Ohio; all we ask, is a continuation of the smiles of the white people as we have hitherto enjoyed them."

Signed, ABRAHAM DANGERFIELD,

JACK HARRIS,

THOMAS ARNOLD,

GEORGE JONES,

JOSEPH KITE.

There were at this time two colored Methodist Churches in Cincinnati—the African M. E. Church, and the M. E. Church,—the latter being the publishers of the above article. The former church was in favor of the repeal of those obnoxious laws, and we continued the circulation of our petition until we got it numerously signed and sent it to the

---

[5] Jacob Wykoff Piatt, born in Kentucky in 1801, was the brother of Donn Piatt, the well-known journalist. J. W. Piatt was a Democrat and an active participant in Cincinnati affairs, crusading with special vigor for a paid, disciplined fire department and winning the hatred of the volunteers, who burned him in effigy. His reforms, however, were carried out before his death in 1857.

[6] See the *Daily Gazette* (Cincinnati), July 4, 1829.

legislature. What became of our petition, or what action the legislature took in the matter, we never found out, but from the position taken by some of our colored brethren, it is likely that the legislature thought best not to interfere in the matter.

During my residence in Cincinnati, I was frequently in the habit of visiting the boats and steamers on the Ohio River, as I was fond of looking at them, especially the machinery. On one of these occasions I visited two boats, and then a third boat which was called the "Criterion." The boats lay close to each other, and on board of the "Criterion" there were thirty slaves bound for the southern market. I was standing on the permanent deck of the "Criterion" when a woman of interesting appearance passed near me, coming from the hurricane deck. I spoke to her and found her name to be Susan Hall, and that she was from the same county where I was born. I had never seen her before, but my mother had often seen her, and spoken of her to me. She told me that she had two children aboard, a boy and a girl. I asked her if she would like to be free. She said she would like it very much. I had to leave off talking with her then, as the watch was very strict, and told her I had to go over into Kentucky, but would return that same night. So great was my abhorrence of slavery, that I was willing to run any risk to accomplish the liberation of a slave. I crossed over into Kentucky, and returned between sundown and dark, and went aboard of the boat. There I remained until about one o'clock, when the woman made her appearance with one of her children. She told me that things were so situated that she could not get her girl without discovery, and we were obliged to leave without the girl. There were two gangways on the boat; one forward and one aft. The gang-plank at the stern was drawn in, and there was no means of exit from the boat except by the forward gang plank. It was impossible, however, for us to escape at that place, as two men were posted there with guns as watch. On looking around, however, I found there was a small boat belonging to the "Criterion," in the water at the stern. I concluded to make use of this boat for the purpose of effecting the escape. I assisted the woman and her boy into the little boat and untied it from the "Criterion." There was another large steamer astern of the "Criterion," and I shot the little boat quickly out under the bow of this other steamer, and made it appear as though I was leaving that steamer instead of the "Criterion." The guards were deluded by this ruse, and paid no attention to us, thinking we came from the other boat. The risk, however, was very great. We could see the barrels of their guns glisten in the moonlight. I effected a landing and brought them to a place of safety. Then I returned and succeeded in getting aboard of the "Criterion" again, and in the same manner I succeeded in effecting the escape of two young men and a young woman.

I found shelter in a safe place in Cincinnati for the woman and child; the others I sent with a guide, to Richmond, Indiana. The woman was pregnant, and remained in Cincinnati till she was in a condition to travel, during which time I paid for her board and sustenance. I then sent her to

Canada, where she married a man named McKinney, and raised a family. One of her sons has often been seen on the streets of Cleveland. His name is Courtney McKinney, and he is a chimney-sweep. He wears on his cap a plate with his name and occupation engraved thereon.

At the time when I effected the escape of the slaves, they were not missed until the next morning, and when they were found to be missing the city was thrown into great commotion, and constables were sent in all directions to search for the missing slaves; but they did not succeed in finding them, nor was I ever suspected.

Chapter Three

O N   T H E 8th day of March, 1829, I married my present wife in Cincinnati, and the next August I moved
to Louisville, Ky., and spent the remainder of the year at
that place working at my trade. From there I moved shortly after to Middletown, nine miles from Louisville, and
worked the next year there at my trade for one Chambers,
the master of my wife's father, who was a slave. In the fall
of the same year I was arrested as a fugitive slave and put in
jail. The jailor procured sufficient aid to handcuff me, and
tried to get a confession from me, having taken off my
clothes, while he stood by with a cowhide in his hand in
order to frighten and intimidate me, but he did not succeed
in getting a confession from me, and he did not whip me
either. I managed to procure bail for my appearance in
Court at the March term, in the sum of $300, but on failure
to prove that I was a slave, I was released from custody by
the Court. The next April I left Louisville for the purpose
of seeking a home for myself and wife in Canada, leaving

my wife in Louisville. When I arrived in Canada I contracted for a small farm, and in the fall of the same year (1831) I returned to Louisville for my wife. In returning from Canada I procured passage aboard of a schooner at Buffalo, and proceeded up the lake, and a storm coming on we were forced to make harbor at Erie, and I concluded not to go by way of Cleveland, as I had first intended, for I thought the vessel was unsafe, but concluded to go by way of Pittsburgh. I started from Erie, and proceeded on foot fourteen miles to a little town called Waterford, in Pennsylvania. At Waterford I purchased some scantling, and built me a small boat 4 x 18. I launched the boat into a stream at Waterford called Lebeef Creek. I went down the creek in my little boat, and out of that creek into another creek, and pursued my way down that second stream until I came to French Creek, and there were a number of mills on French Creek, and dams were built across from one side to the other, and at some of those dams there were shutes, so that boats could pass through. Where there were no shutes I had to draw my boat out of the water, and drag it to places below the dam. There were great hills on both sides of French Creek, and the growth of the timber, which was principally hemlock, was very thick, and in the daytime it was so dark I could scarcely see my way through.

While proceeding down French Creek I was quite amused to see the Indians gathering the crude petroleum which was floating on top of the water. They gathered the oil by spreading blankets over the surface of the water, and allowing them to soak up the oil, and then they would take the blankets, and wring the oil out into vessels which they procured for that purpose. What they did with the oil I do not know.[1]

Proceeding on, I arrived at the mouth of French Creek to a small town, (the name of which I have forgotten,) and from thence into the Allegheny River and down to Pittsburgh. I disposed of my boat at Pittsburgh, and with the proceeds I paid my passage to Cincinnati. My wife met me in Cincinnati, and then we started up the Ohio River as far as Portsmouth, Ohio, with what little household goods we had. My object was to reach Chillicothe, to which point the Ohio Canal had been completed, and then travel by way of the canal. I hired a team to take us and our goods to Chillicothe, and from there we traveled on the canal to Newark, in Licking county. By this time cold weather had set in, and we were compelled to spend the winter in Newark.

In the following April, the canal being again open, we proceeded on our journey, and arrived in Cleveland the same month. There was very little communication between the United States and Canada in those days, so we waited in Cleveland for a good opportunity to cross over into Canada, and finding no opportunity in Cleveland we went to Buffalo, where we stayed a few days. Here my wife became greatly troubled in consequence of having left her father, and it lay so heavily upon her that she gave me no rest. Seeing her unwillingness to go to Canada, and her

---

[1] They drank it as a medicine.

fears that she would never see her father again, I concluded to give up the farm, and my wife having taken a fancy to Cleveland, we determined to go back and settle there. We accordingly came to Cleveland, and I sought employment at my trade. But my color was an obstacle and I could not get work of that kind. I managed, however, to obtain employment as cook on the schooner Aurora, that sailed on the lakes between Mackinaw and Buffalo, and I kept that position for three months. Leonard Case, Sr.,[2] and P. B. Andrews,[3] of Cleveland, had built a steam mill at the same spot where the C.& P.R.R. shops now stand,[4] and Mr. J. H. Hudson, who was part owner of the vessel on which I was employed, purchased that mill from Case and Andrews. The mill was operated during the day, and he wanted to run it also during the night. Mr. Hudson applied to me to act as engineer during part of the time. A man by the name of Erastus Smith and his son Washington were running the engine at the time. I was perfectly ignorant of running an engine, and had no knowledge of machinery, nor of steam power, and Mr. Hudson requested Mr. Erastus Smith to in-

---

[2] Leonard Case, Sr. (1786-1864), pioneer Cleveland lawyer, banker, and land speculator, was one of Cleveland's wealthiest early citizens. Shortly before Malvin's arrival he had been president of the village of Cleveland, but by the 1830's he had given up public life for private pursuits.

[3] Philip B. Andrews was a charter member of Cleveland's First Presbyterian Church (now the Old Stone Church on Public Square) and was an early local industrialist.

[4] On River Street, now W. 11th, near the mouth of the Cuyahoga River.

50

struct me how to run the engine. On the day appointed at 12 o'clock I took charge of the engine. Mr. Smith and his son that same day took their guns and went out in the woods to hunt. They were gone nearly two hours, and when they returned I heard Washington ask his father some question which I did not comprehend, but the answer I understood very well. The engine was running at a very rapid rate, and the blue streaks of steam were passing through the joints of the boiler. Mr. Smith answered, "I don't care if he blows her to h——." I immediately sprang to the safety valve, opened it, and let the steam blow off, for from his answer I knew there was something wrong; then I left immediately and came to town, and I reported what had occurred to P. B. Andrews, the gentleman who had built the engine. He sent an engineer down to the mill to see into the matter, and, on examination, he found that there was only four inches of water in the boilers, and that the supply cock was shut off, so that no water could get into the boilers at all. I did not know how the boilers were supplied with water. Mr. Smith or his son must have shut it off before they went to the woods. The engineer instructed me how to supply the boilers, and we got things all right and started again. After this the mill was only run during the day, and at night I would take a portion of the engine apart, lay each piece separate from the other, so that I would make no mistake, and, in like manner, repeat my work at different times until I had taken the whole engine apart and put it together again, and I become [*sic*] complete master of the machinery.

I ran that engine twelve or thirteen months, and then I communicated to Mr. Hudson a project I had formed of buying my father-in-law's freedom. I opened correspondence with his master, and he replied that he would take $400.00 for the old man, who was then sixty years of age, and that he would take $100.00 down, and the balance on time. I got a subscription paper and circulated it, and upon that subscription paper the public kindly donated $100.00. I then made two notes, payable in one and two years, for $150.00 each, and procured the endorsement thereon of John M. Sterling, Sr.,[5] Deacon Benjamin Rouse,[6] Judith Richmond, and Thomas Whelpley.[7] I sent my wife to Kentucky with the money and notes, and on paying the

---

[5] John M. Sterling was a real-estate developer, streetcar promoter, pillar of the First Presbyterian Church, and a pioneer Cleveland abolitionist. In 1837 he helped draft the constitution of the Cuyahoga Anti-Slavery Society, which declared, in part, that the goal of the society was not only the abolition of slavery in the South but also "the elevation of our colored brethren to their proper rank as men."

[6] Originally a builder in Massachusetts, Benjamin Rouse gave up business to serve as a Western agent for the American Sunday School Union. Finding Cleveland sadly in need of formal religion, he settled there, establishing the city's first Sunday school on the Public Square. (The lot he purchased for this purpose cost him about $600 but by the time of his death its value was estimated at $80,000, "thus amply repaying Mr. Rouse," according to a pious early chronicler, "for his labors in the cause of religion and morality.") Rouse was a deacon in the First Baptist Church, Malvin's congregation, using his skill in the building trade to help in the construction of the church.

[7] A resident of Ohio City (as Cleveland's West Side was then

$100.00 and delivering the notes, her father was released, and came with her to Cleveland.

Hon. Samuel Williamson[8] was the attorney for my father-in-law's master, and the notes, as they became due, were sent to Mr. Williamson for collection. Not being able to pay the first note, I was sued in the County Court. I expostulated with Mr. Williamson, and tried to be released from the obligation, to some extent at least. He replied to me, that though he was opposed to slavery, yet when a person agreed to pay money, it was morally wrong to refuse to do it. Judgment was rendered against me on the note, and I continued to work until I paid the notes.

My wife's father, whose name was Caleb Dorsey,[9] lived in Cleveland fifteen years after his freedom was obtained, when, becoming anxious to visit his children in Louisville, he so informed my wife. We both protested against his going, as we thought the old man would not be able to chance the journey. Notwithstanding our entreaties, he persisted in going. He left Cleveland on a Friday, arriving in Louisville on Saturday night. The next day being Sabbath, he went to Church. On the same night he took the

---

known), Thomas Whelpley was elected, in 1836, recorder of Ohio City in that town's first election.

[8] Samuel Williamson, prominent banker, lawyer, and judge, played an early part in Cleveland municipal affairs, serving on the first board of trustees of the village in 1815 and later acting as Treasurer and as a member of the Board of School Managers.

[9] The city directory for 1848-49 lists Caleb Dorsey's occupation as "wood sawer."

53

cholera, and died, at the age of seventy-five years.

During the first years of my residence in Cleveland, and while I was in the employ of Mr. Hudson, there was a little brick building on Academy Lane,[10] owned by one Mr. Brewster, and which he allowed the congregation of the First Baptist Church, then organized, to use as a place of meeting and worship. I had, while in Cincinnati, obtained a license to preach the Gospel, from the Enon Baptist Church, and when I came to Cleveland, I occasionally preached for the First Baptist Church in the building on Academy Lane. I often received invitations to preach in the country, sometimes at Rockport, sometimes at Euclid, and other towns. My wife and myself have remained members of the Baptist Church ever since we were in Cleveland, and are still members thereof.

------

[10] Now W. 4th Street.

Chapter Four

THE EXTREMITY to which I had been driven, to pay the notes which I had given for the freedom of my wife's father, obliged me to resort to some means of earning the money to pay them. My earnings while in Mr. Hudson's employ, were barely sufficient to support my family. Through the kindness of Mr. James S. Clark,[1] I was enabled to purchase, on easy terms, a vessel owned by Abraham Wright of Rockport. When I went to take out a license, the deputy Collector refused to grant it, deciding that my color was an obstacle. But when the Collector him-

---

[1] James S. Clark (or Clarke) was an active railroad and real-estate promoter. In the latter capacity, he helped precipitate the comic-opera "Bridge War" between Cleveland and Ohio City in 1837, an incident which led Cleveland to the brink of bombarding and besieging its rival across the river. Clark was also concerned with the plight of the Negro and in 1827 was the secretary of the newly-organized Cuyahoga County branch of the American Colonization Society. This organization believed that there was no place for the free Negro in America and advocated his settle-

self arrived, who was the Hon. Samuel Starkweather,[2] well known to all the citizens of Cleveland, he decided that I had as much right to own and sail a vessel upon the lakes as I had to own a horse and buggy and drive through the streets, and he granted me a license. My vessel was called "The Grampus." After I obtained my license, Mr. Diodate Clark employed me to carry limestone and cedar posts from Kelley's and surrounding islands. I earned money enough to pay up the notes. I then disposed of the vessel.

My next employment was on the First Baptist Church, then on the corner of Champlain and Seneca streets,[3] the place now occupied by the U. S. Organ Company. When the church was built and ready for dedication, the question was raised among the members as to where the colored people should sit. There was a diversity of opinion on the subject. In the first place, it was proposed to finish off the

---

ment in Liberia. It is somewhat curious that, in spite of the society's anti-Negro position, an active member, such as Clark, would befriend Malvin rather than urge him to emigrate to Africa.

[2] A well-known Cleveland political figure, Samuel Starkweather was a local power in the Democratic Party during the Jacksonian era. Thrice elected mayor of Cleveland (1844, 1845, and 1857), he was also a judge, a railroad promoter, a friend of the public schools, and a popular orator.

[3] Malvin and his wife, Harriet, were among the charter members of the First Baptist Church upon its organization in 1833. The building on Seneca and Champlain Streets was finished in 1836, becoming a source of pride to Ohio Baptists and a Cleveland landmark because of its towering spire. The site is now occupied by the Terminal Group.

pews in the gallery in the same style as in the auditorium, and that I should have the finishing of it under my control and management; but finding that too expensive, they abandoned the method, and it was next proposed to the colored members that before the sale of the pews took place, that I and one Stephen Griffin[4] might make a selection of half a dozen pews anywhere in the church that might be suitable, whether on the broad or side aisle, or in front of the pulpit. To that I objected, stating that if I had to be colonized, I preferred to be colonized at Liberia, rather than in the House of God; that Christ or the Apostles never made any distinction on account of race or color. It was, however, decided that the colored people should sit in the gallery. On every proper occasion thereafter at church meetings I would bring up the question of the distinction of color in the house of worship, and the members became nearly divided on the question, and after struggling for eighteen months, it was finally concluded that the colored people should have the privilege of obtaining pews in any part of the building, as other persons, and my object was thus accomplished.

---

[4] Stephen Griffin, a Negro mason.

Chapter Five

DURING THE YEAR 1839 I was employed as a hand on the steamboat "Rochester," plying between Buffalo and Chicago. The following year I left this position, and purchased a canal boat from S.R. Hutchinson & Co. This firm owned the stone mill on the canal in Cleveland. My boat, which was called the "Auburn," was engaged in conveying wheat and merchandise on the Ohio Canal. The boat was a good passenger packet, with good cabins, and her former owners concluded to buy the boat back, which they did. They then employed me as captain, to manage her. On one occasion, while I was running the boat, after having loaded with merchandise, I was ordered to deliver the goods at Chillicothe. Leaving Cleveland about noon, we arrived at Niles about nine o'clock in the evening. At this place we were hailed by some person saying that a passenger wanted to get aboard to go south. We came alongside the dock and landed. Pretty soon after some baggage came on board, and in a short time the owner of the baggage, who was a female, appeared.

My crew consisted of one white steersman, one colored steersman, two white drivers, one colored bowman, and one colored female cook. When the lady arrived I stood aboard of the stern deck and assisted her aboard. When she went down into the cabin and saw the colored cook, she was taken completely by surprise. The colored steersman just then happened to go down into the cabin after something. The lady was sitting on the locker, and when she saw the colored steersman she went immediately to the other side of the boat. After the bowman had got his lines snugly curled, he went down into the cabin, and she accosted him, saying that she would like to see the captain. Accordingly, I was called and went down to see what she wanted. The light shone in my face so that she could easily see my features. The lady, after seeing me, suddenly sprang to her feet, and with great shortness of breath exclaimed, "Well, I never! well, I never! well, I never." I made a bow and left her, and ordered the cook to set her state-room doors open, and to take off all the bedding from the middle berth, and supply clean bedding from the locker, so that she might see that the bedding was changed, and I requested the cook to tell the surprised lady to take the middle berth. She refused to go to bed, and sat up all night.

We arrived at Lock 21, north end of the Akron locks, at midnight. At nearly every lock there was a house or grocery, and I instructed the crew to keep the blinds on the boat closed, so that the lady should not know she was in a village; for, seeing that she was afraid of colored people, I wanted to give her full opportunity of getting acquainted with them before she arrived at her home in Circleville. We arrived at Lock 1 a little after daylight; that brought us on the Wolf Creek level. On going into the Wolf Creek lock, seeing that the lock was ready, we ran the boat right into the lock, and the hands divided, a part on one side of the boat, and a part on the other side. I gave the driver the signal, and he opened the wicket, lowered the boat down, and the lady was prevented from getting off there, if she had felt disposed to do so. When we came to the Fulton lock we pursued the same course as at the former lock. Before we had got to this point, and while we were yet on the Wolf Creek level, I invited the lady to breakfast, which she refused, saying that she did not feel very well. When we arrived at the Fulton Lock, it brought us to the Massillon level, and it being dinner time, I invited the lady to dinner. She still complained of not feeling very well, but took a piece of pie from where she stood. Then we arrived at the Bethlehem level, and when tea was ready, I invited her to tea, and she took a cup of tea and a biscuit.

Just about this time we passed through a strip of woods about a mile in length. The moon was full, and it was a beautiful evening. The cook, having got through with her cabin work, came on deck. While she was proceeding towards the deck, the lady passenger followed her in a hesitating manner. They promenaded the deck together for a while, and then retired. I suppose the lady took a good night's sleep, for I did not hear anything from her until

61

the next morning. When breakfast was ready, on receiving an invitation, she readily took a seat at the table, and ate a hearty meal, and from that time on she felt reconciled to her surroundings, and conversed freely with the cook and all on board. When we arrived at Circleville she left us. I provided means for the conveyance of her baggage, and on her leaving she thanked me, and said, "Captain, when I first came aboard your boat, not being accustomed to travel in this way, I supposed I must have acted quite awkward. Now, I must return my thanks to you and your crew, for the kind treatment I have received. I never traveled so comfortably in all my life, and I expect to go north soon, and I will defer my journey until you are going north, even if I am obliged to wait two or three days." I never saw the lady again after that.

Chapter Six

PRIOR TO THE time that I was engaged as captain on the canal boat as narrated, and during the time I was acting in the capacity of engineer for Mr. Hudson, I had taken considerable interest in the question of the education of the colored children.[1] About the year 1832 I

---

[1] When Malvin first organized his school, Negroes could count on no aid from the state. In a school law passed in 1829 the legislature was careful to insist "that nothing in this act . . . shall be so construed as to permit black or mulatto persons to attend the schools hereby established." Negroes had to rely upon self-help or public charity to support their meager schools. The Ohio legislature did not authorize public schools for Negroes until the session of 1847-48, but this law (and a modification passed the next session) proved totally inadequate to meet the problem, since it provided that Negro schools be supported from taxes on Negro property. Since few Negroes owned much property, the revenue from this source was insufficient to provide for anything resembling adequate schooling. Consequently, by 1850, only one out of every ten Negroes was attending school in Ohio, as compared with one out of every six in Massachusetts. Almost

called a meeting of the colored men of Cleveland, and among others John Brown, Alexander Bowman, and David Smith. Mr. John H. Hudson gave us the use of a room on the mill premises to keep school in for colored children, and at that meeting we hired a half breed to teach the children, paying him $20 a month,[2] and he taught for us three months; when he left we hired a young lady by the name

---

one-fifth of Ohio's Negro population was illiterate, as opposed to one-eleventh in Massachusetts. In 1852 the basis was laid for an adequate (though segregated) Negro public school system. The key provision of that law placed taxes from Negro property in a common fund with revenue from white taxation. The disbursement of funds to the schools was to be made solely on the basis of the number of children, regardless of their color. By 1860, under this system Ohio Negroes enjoyed educational opportunities comparable to those in any state in the Union. Over one-sixth of the state's colored population was attending school in that year, and the Negro schools were beginning to approach the quality of the common schools.

In Cleveland the education of Negro children was conducted haphazardly for a decade following the opening of Malvin's school, with various struggling schoolhouses competing for private charity. In 1843, however, the Cleveland City Council began to subsidize the Negro schools out of the general revenue, even though this was not required by law. By the 1850's Cleveland had abolished segregated schools entirely, and colored children attended the public schools on the same basis as their white neighbors. Cleveland even had a Negro school teacher, teaching predominantly white classes.

[2] An ample salary by the standards of the day. Twenty years later, in the 1850's, salaries for male teachers in white public schools averaged between $25 and $28 per month, and salaries for teachers in the Negro schools were thoroughly competitive.

of Clarissa Wright as teacher. Her parents lived in Talmadge, Ohio, and she taught about two months and a-half, when, in consequences of her mother's sickness, she had to leave. Then we employed a man by the name of M. M. Clark, from the East. I don't think he taught over three months. While he was teaching I called a meeting of colored men and suggested to them the propriety of calling a State convention of colored men, which was done, and, as far as I know, it was the first colored convention ever known in the United States; at least I never had heard of one before.[3] After having agreed upon calling the convention we proposed for that purpose to employ Mr. Clark, our then school teacher, to canvass the State, and lecture to the colored people on the propriety of calling a State convention. He done so, and the State convention in 1835 was called in the City of Columbus as a consequence of our effort, and that convention organized itself into what was then called "the School Fund Society." The business and object of that was to establish schools in different parts of the State for colored children. We established one in Cincinnati, one in Columbus, one in Springfield, and another in Cleveland, and that convention decided to employ M. M. Clark as an agent to raise funds for the support of the schools. The first donation was by James S. Clark, Esq., and in canvassing the State the good citizens of the State responded to the call. We kept these schools going for

---

[3] Malvin is mistaken. The first Negro convention was held in Philadelphia in September of 1830.

about two years, and several of the adult colored people of Cleveland, not having had the benefits of education before extended to them, went to the schools established in Cleveland, and learned to read and write pretty well. A gentleman, whose name I do not now remember, but who lived in the southern part of the State, donated for the support of these schools a tract of twenty-five acres.

I was not satisfied, however, as long as the black laws remained on the statute books, which prohibited colored children from going to the public schools, and being anxious for their repeal, in common with many of the colored people of the State I called another meeting of the colored people of Cleveland, and suggested the propriety of circulating a petition to be sent to the Legislature for the repeal of those odious laws, and I also proposed that we employ some lecturers to lecture through the State and raise a sentiment in favor of the repeal of those laws. We accordingly employed John L. Watson,[4] of Cleveland, William H. Day,[5] of Oberlin, and R. R. Chancellor, of Chillicothe, for

---

[4] Cleveland Negro barber and bathhouse proprietor whose establishment was advertised as the most luxurious west of New York. A militant spokesman for the Free Negro, John L. Watson served as president of the 1850 Ohio Colored Men's Convention held at Cincinnati.

[5] William Howard Day, Negro newspaperman, graduated from Oberlin College and worked in Cleveland on the staff of the *Daily True Democrat* and as a librarian for the Cleveland Library Association. In 1853 he was editor of the short-lived newspaper, *The Aliened American*, Cleveland's first Negro journal. In 1854, Day, then a reporter, was expelled from the reporters'

that purpose, and shortly after they were employed they
obtained permission to lecture in the State House at Columbus, and we found good results ensued from the lectures. I
don't exactly remember the year, but I think it was in 1844.
The Legislature was then Democratic, and Hon. Franklin
T. Backus[6] was elected to the Legislature, and it was
through his efforts in our behalf, and the effect those lectures had on the people that the black laws were repealed,
with the exception of the school law prohibiting colored
children from going to the public schools.[7]

---

gallery of the Ohio Senate because of his color. In 1859, John
Brown entrusted Day with the secret job of printing a constitution for the Negro republic he planned to create after his raid
on Harper's Ferry.

[6] Franklin T. Backus (1813-70), corporation lawyer, active in
the Whig Party, and elected to the Ohio Legislature in 1846 and
the Ohio Senate in 1848. His hatred of slavery and his sympathy with the plight of the Negro led Backus to volunteer as
a lawyer for the defense in the celebrated Oberlin-Wellington
rescue case in 1859.

[7] The repeal of the "Black Laws," in January of 1849, was not so
much the result of triumphant idealism or enlightened public
opinion (as Malvin implies) as it was the simple consequence
of a deal, in the classic American political tradition. The close
elections of 1848 had left the Ohio House deadlocked, with
neither the Whigs nor Democrats able to organize the House
or elect a United States senator without the support of members
of the Free Soil Party. That minor party was itself divided into
factions, but after much complicated party maneuvering two
key Free Soilers threw their support to the Democrats, enabling
them to control the lower house. The Democrats, in return,
supported the anti-slavery spokesman, Salmon P. Chase, for Senator (in preference to the even more abolitionist Joshua Gid-

About the year 1843 a couple of slaves ran away from Tennessee,[8] and were recommended here to one Henry Jackson, a barber, who was reputed to be an abolitionist, and they stayed here under his protection from four to six weeks. During that time he learned where they were from, and the names of their owners. A reward having been offered for their apprehension, Jackson communicated that fact to H. V. Wilson [*sic*],[9] who afterwards became Judge

---

dings) and also voted to repeal the Black Laws. Thus, what years of agitation and moral exhortation had failed to accomplish was settled in a few weeks of political horse-trading.

[8] This incident took place in 1841, not 1843. Until this time fugitives from slavery had been captured and returned from Cleveland more or less routinely, without creating much of a stir. Public opinion was firmly against abolitionism and eager to appease the South. The initial public reaction to this case was to view with disfavor and even to threaten the defenders of the runaways. Partly because of the underhanded tactics employed in this case to lure the slaves back, a reaction began to set in at this time. Cleveland was on its way towards becoming a center of abolitionism, and this case played a part in creating that sentiment. From this time on, until the case of Lucy Bagby (discussed below), it was the proud boast of Clevelanders that no slave could be returned to bondage from Cuyahoga County.

[9] Hiram V. Willson (1808-66), Cleveland jurist, as a young man studied law with Francis Scott Key. Moving to Cleveland, he formed a successful partnership with Harry B. Payne, a fellow Democrat. When Payne retired from law, Willson took as his partner Edward Wade, an abolitionist. In 1852 they both ran for Congress, and Wade, the Free Soiler, defeated his partner. In 1855, Willson was appointed federal judge for the newly-created Northern District of Ohio. As judge he presided over the famous Oberlin-Wellington slave rescue case, as well as the

of the U. S. District Court in Cleveland. Jackson could not write, but he engaged Mr. Wilson to open a correspondence with the owners of the two men. At least I concluded, from the fact that Jackson could not write, and all the circumstances, that Mr. Wilson did the writing.

After the fugitives had been in Cleveland about six weeks they left and went to Buffalo, and shortly after the agent of the owners arrived in Cleveland. Learning from Jackson that the boys were in Buffalo there was a consultation held between Mr. Wilson, Jackson and the agent, and it was concluded to get the men back to Cleveland, or in Ohio, for the reason that colored men were allowed to testify in the State of New York, but could not testify in Ohio. The black laws had not yet been repealed. They planned that Jackson, the agent, and Mr. Wilson, should go to Buffalo, and that Jackson should be their spokesman. The names of the two boys were Alexander Williams and John Houston. Before they went to Buffalo, Williams applied to J. F. Hanks, who was a portrait painter, to become an apprentice, but Hanks did not employ him, and Jackson, as spokesman for the trio, on their arrival in Buffalo, represented to Williams that Mr. Hanks had agreed to employ him as apprentice, and had sent him down to see him (Williams,) to have him come back to Cleveland and enter into the apprenticeship, and he represented to John Houston, who was formerly a cook in the South, that there

---

case of Lucy Bagby, discussed by Malvin later. Despite his association with the Democratic Party, Willson vigorously supported the Union during the Civil War.

was a new brig just launched in Cleveland, and the Captain had employed him to engage a cook, and so he had come to Buffalo to have him ship on board of the new brig as cook.

Before leaving Cleveland for Buffalo there had been a warrant issued and placed in the hands of Madison Miller, who was Sheriff, that was to be served on the boys as soon as they landed in Cleveland. By reason of the representations thus made to the boys they were induced to return to Cleveland. They no sooner landed than they were arrested and placed in jail. A crowd of colored people, myself among the number, gathered around the jail late, in order to see that they were not run off during the night without a chance of hearing. Charles Stetson, Esq., kindly volunteered his services gratis as attorney for the boys, and we employed to assist him Thomas Bolton, Esq.,[10] who was a

---

[10] Although Thomas Bolton settled in Cleveland in 1834, only a year after his graduation from Harvard, he rapidly made a name for himself in local affairs. He helped draft the first city charter in 1835 and was elected councilman and, later, alderman. In 1841, when the incident took place, Bolton was prosecuting attorney and a staunch Democrat. The jailed Negro boys had been held incommunicado, and their lawyer, Edward Wade, had been denied access to them because of his abolitionist views. When Bolton, a Democrat, took the case, the jailer allowed him to see the prisoners and prepare a defense. Despite public indignation and actual threats of violence, Bolton persisted in the case, helping to swing public opinion in northern Ohio against slavery. In 1848 Bolton left the Democratic Party for the Free Soil Party and in 1856 lent his support to the new Republican Party. Elected a judge that same year, he held office until his retirement in 1866.

Democrat. We paid Mr. Bolton $25 to take the case. The agent, Mr. Lindenberger, employed H. B. Payne, Esq.,[11] and Hon. Horace Toole, and so the boys, in a day or two, were brought before Judge Barber,[12] (not the present Judge Barber).

When the boys were brought out and it was ascertained how they were deceived and brought back from Buffalo, Edward Wade, Esq.,[13] interposed a motion to the court ask-

---

[11] Henry B. Payne, one of Cleveland's most successful lawyers and politicians, came to Cleveland in 1832, entering into law partnership with Hiram V. Willson. He was active in all phases of Cleveland affairs and was, in 1851, elected to the Ohio Senate. That same year he won the Democrats' nomination for United States Senate, narrowly losing the election to Ben Wade. In 1857, he was the Democratic candidate for governor but again narrowly missed the prize, this time to Salmon P. Chase, by a few hundred votes. In 1874, he was elected to Congress, and at the Republican Convention of 1880 he made a strong but unsuccessful bid for the Presidential nomination. Elected to the United States Senate in 1884, he died in 1896.

Payne was never a friend of the Negro. In 1857, while running for governor, he assailed the Negroes of Cleveland as "poor, miserable, worthless creatures." His subsequent narrow defeat was attributed by some to the Negro vote in Cleveland, which helped supply Chase's margin of victory.

[12] Josiah Barber, lawyer, land speculator, and industrialist, was one of the original vice-presidents of the Cuyahoga County Colonization Society and was the first mayor of Ohio City in 1837.

[13] In addition to his involvement in other philanthropies and causes, Edward Wade was the first president of the Cuyahoga Anti-Slavery Society upon its organization in 1837 and remained an active agent in the Underground Railroad. In 1841, when he tried to defend the runaway boys, all sorts of obstacles were

ing for a continuance of the cause for twelve days. It was
the law that when a fugitive slave was arrested and put in
jail or custody, that if he could furnish bail of $1,000, he
would be released from prison until the expiration of the
time of adjournment. So Alexander Bowman, John
Brown[14] and myself furnished the required bail. Then I
took the boy Alexander Williams from the jail and went
with him to Buffalo by the advice of the lawyers, to ascer-
tain the particulars in the case. I had a letter from Mr. Bolton, directed to George A. Barker, Esq., the Prosecuting
Attorney at Buffalo. I arrived in Buffalo about six o'clock
in the evening. Mr. H. B. Payne took passage on the same
boat and was on his way to New York. I went to Mr. Barker's office and presented the letter. Mr. Barker informed
me that on the same boat I came down on in the mail there
was a letter from H. B. Payne. He read it to me, and it was
in substance, if not the precise words, as follows:

"GEORGE A. BARKER, ESQ.:

"There were two runaway negroes taken up in Cleveland (naming the day), much to the satisfaction of all the

---

put in his way, but public opinion soon swung around to his
point of view, and he was elected to Congress to represent
Cleveland from 1852 to 1861.

[14] John Brown, the barber, was one of Cleveland's oldest and most
prominent Negro settlers. Born in Virginia, of free parents, he
came to Cleveland in 1828. A crusty, argumentative defender
of Negro rights, Brown became a well-known local "character,"
even appearing in some of Artemus Ward's humorous sketches.
He was the stepfather-in-law of William H. Day. At his death,
in 1869, he left an estate of almost $40,000, mostly in real estate.

citizens of Cleveland, except a few black abolitionists and a few white negroes. I expect to go to New York in a day or two, and defer action until I see you."

Mr. Barker then said to me: "I am well acquainted with Thomas Bolton, a brother Democrat." So that night he had a jury called, and Alexander Williams was called in before the jury and testified as to the manner in which they were decoyed. The jury decided that these men were kidnapped, and Mr. Barker that same night wrote a letter to the Governor of New York for a requisition on the Governor of Ohio for the men that kidnapped the boys, and Mr. Barker requested me to call at his office the next morning at 8 o'clock. I came to his office at the appointed time, and had not been there over ten minutes, when who should come in but Mr. H. B. Payne. Mr. Payne and I did not say much to each other. He appeared a little confused to see me. Mr. Barker handed me a letter to give to Mr. Bolton, and so I returned that morning with Alexander Williams by steamer, and when we arrived in Cleveland I delivered the prisoner to the authorities, and he was returned back to jail. A day or two after the requisition was forwarded to the Governor of Ohio for the arrest of Jackson, the agent of Lindenberger, and H. V. Wilson, to answer the charge as found by the jury for kidnapping. The officer in charge of the requisition went to Columbus and presented his papers to the Governor, who issued a warrant for the arrest of the persons named. Jackson, having heard of this, ran away, as also did Lindenberger, so that when the day of trial of the boys came they were not present. The trial, however, had not come off, and one day, as I happened to go to a meeting, on my return about half past nine in the evening there was a rap at my door, and when I opened it, I found to my surprise Alexander Williams. I hardly knew what to do with Williams. My home was then on the corner of Bond[15] and York, (now Hamilton) street, which was then in the woods. I dared not harbor him in my house, so I took him to the woods five or six rods off and had him climb a tree till I could find a place of safety. One Deacon Hamlin was building a one-story brick house on Prospect street, which was enclosed but not finished. I got some comforters and Buffalo robes, and placed them in the building, and then I went back to the wood after Williams, but I had lost track of the tree he was in, and wandered about, afraid to call, lest I should be heard by some one. After considerable search I found the tree, had him come down, and took him to the building, and kept him there for several days. His complexion was a bright mulatto. I made a composition, and painted all the visible parts of the man, and made a very black man of him, so he walked about the streets of Cleveland boldly and no one recognized him as Alexander Williams. He afterwards left Cleveland for New York State, and, perhaps, went into Canada. On the day of trial the other boy, John Houston, was brought into Court, but Jackson and Lindenberger not being at the trial, there was no one to appear against the boy, and he was discharged.

---

[15] Now E. 6th Street.

Chapter Seven

THE ESTABLISHMENT of colored schools in Ohio, in which I had taken an active part as already stated, made a decided improvement in the condition of the colored people, but like other people who have not had the benefits of education, there were many among them who were not from the force of circumstances over honest. Reform of course was needed, and I undertook in every way possible to do whatever I could towards improvement and advancement of my people in this respect. Very often, when charges were brought against colored men, I would go their bail, in order that they might have a fair opportunity to prepare for trial and test the truth of the charge, and being a property owner, I was called upon in many cases for bail, which I seldom refused. On one occasion, when Hon. Samuel Starkweather was Judge of the Court of Common Pleas, a colored man by the name of Archie Lorton was arrested for horse stealing, and I went his bail. Shortly after I bailed him, he packed up his things and ran away to

Canada. As soon as I ascertained where he was, I employed Deputy Sheriff S. P. Bosworth to go with me to Canada and arrest and bring him back. We went to Detroit and crossed over into Windsor, and thence proceeded to London, where I got track of him. I found that he was at a little town called Waterford, twelve miles west of London. We proceeded to a magistrate in London in order to procure a warrant for his arrest. The magistrate claimed that he had no jurisdiction in the matter, and referred me to another magistrate, who again referred me to what they called the high magistrate. I went to the high magistrate, and he also refused to issue a warrant, for the reason that he had no jurisdiction in the matter. I then went and employed a lawyer, and the lawyer went with me to the high magistrate and demanded a warrant; and after convincing the magistrate that he was justified in issuing a warrant, it was granted. We then proceeded to Waterford and arrested Lorton a little after dark, and then put up at the American Hotel. The Bailiff left the prisoner in my charge, and I kept watch over him all night, and the next morning the Bailiff took him out of my hands and placed him in jail, and reported to the Mayor of the city, who ordered the prisoner to be brought before him on Monday morning at 9 o'clock. On our way to the Mayor's office he shouted that he was a slave, and that we were kidnappers and were taking him back into slavery. In a few minutes we were surrounded by forty or fifty infuriated colored men, and we expected every moment that they would mob us. The deputy undertook to pacify them, but they would not listen to him, and at length

I succeeded in getting them to hear me. I told them how the matter was, and they believed my statement, and some of them exclaimed that if he was a horse thief they did not want him there, and were glad to see him removed.

Lorton, having left this [*sic*] wife in Waterford, he then and there agreed that if we would go back to Waterford and meet his wife, that he would go with us to Port Stanley without a hearing. We consented to do this and started toward Waterford, and on the way we met the stage coming towards London with the prisoner's wife. We stopped the stage, and upon her statement that she had left something behind, and that she must go back to Waterford, I agreed to take her place in the stage, and that she should take my place in the carriage with the bailiff. They were to proceed on to Waterford, and the prisoner promised if that was done he would go back to the United States without insisting on a trial in Canada.

I took her place in the stage accordingly, and took charge of her baggage, which I checked to Detroit. I agreed to take the railroad and meet the party at Lobi Station, the first station after leaving London for Windsor. I met them at Lobi Station as agreed on, and then the prisoner refused to accompany us to the United States, which I had in part anticipated. Then we had to go back to London and after we arrived there, the Mayor ordered him to be put in jail till I could get a requisition, limiting the time to three weeks. I then went home, and proceeded at once to Columbus and called on Governor Medill. He said that he had no jurisdiction outside of the United States, and therefore could not

77

grant a requisition, but referred me to the Secretary of State. Samuel Williamson, Esq., who was then Prosecuting Attorney in Cleveland, at my request, wrote a letter to the Secretary of State, and the reply of the Secretary of State was, that horse stealing was grand larceny, and did not come within the category of the Ashburton Treaty, and that he had no jurisdiction to issue a requisition in the matter. I was therefore left without any remedy, and had been put to great expense in attempting to bring Lorton back.[1]

Some time afterwards, Lorton committed some depredation in Canada and fled to Adrian, Michigan, and as soon as I heard of his being there, I got the necessary requisition from the Governor, and had him arrested and brought to Cleveland. He was tried, convicted, and sent to the penitentiary for seven years.

---

[1] Archy Lorton (or Lanton) was successful in imposing his story upon the sympathetic but credulous Canadians. The case, which occurred in 1856, was later cited as an example of the lengths to which slave-catchers would go to return their victims to bondage. Basing his account on a thoroughly garbled version of the case that appeared in the Toronto *Globe* of December 24, 1860, a twentieth-century historian maintained that Lorton was "spirited away and probably taken back to slavery." He concluded that this was "the only case on record where the Canadian law did not protect a fugitive." In view of Malvin's more reliable, first-hand testimony, this solitary blemish on Canada's record can now be removed. (See Fred Landon, "Social Conditions Among the Negroes in Upper Canada Before 1865," *Ontario Historical Society, Papers and Records*, XXII [1925], p. 155.)

Chapter Eight

I WILL STATE a circumstance that may perhaps be of some interest, that occurred shortly before the war: A young colored girl ran away from Wheeling, Va., and came to Cleveland, and took up her residence in the family of Mr. W. E. Ambush.[1] After she remained there a short period of time, it was ascertained by her owners as to her whereabouts, and they came to Cleveland in search of her.

---

[1] The case of the runaway, Lucy Bagby, was tried in January of 1861, during the interval between the secession of the Gulf States and the outbreak of the Civil War, a time when segments of northern public opinion were inclined to appease southern grievances in the hope of averting war. Lucy had the unfortunate distinction of being the last runaway slave ever returned to the South under the provisions of the Fugitive Slave Law. The contrast between the earlier runaway case (discussed above) and the case of Lucy is a striking one. In 1841, violence had been threatened against those who *defended* the runaways. Twenty years later, more than one hundred fifty Federal soldiers were needed to prevent the Cleveland mob from setting Lucy free.

The girl went by the name of Lucy, and she had sought employment in the family of George A. Benedict, and she left Ambush and went to Benedict's. As soon as her owners, who were father and son, named Goshorn, arrived in Cleveland, they obtained a warrant for the girl's arrest, which was placed in the hands of Seth A. Abbey, then United States Marshal, and she was arrested by him and placed in the county jail. A number of the citizens of Cleveland immediately employed Hon. R. P. Spalding[2] on behalf of the girl, and she was taken out of the custody of the Marshal, on a write of *habeas corpus* issued by Judge Tilden, Probate Judge of Cuyahoga County. When they were ready for hearing, Judge Tilden inquired of Mr. Spalding whether he desired the prisoner to be brought into his court. Judge Spalding replied that the investigation could proceed without her presence. Thereupon, after a hearing had [been held], Judge Tilden remanded her back again into the custody of the Marshal, who kept her in jail.

She was brought before Judge Wilson [*sic*], U. S. Dis-

---

[2] Rufus P. Spalding, Ohio lawyer and politician. Before coming to Cleveland he had represented Summit County in the Ohio legislature, where he had distinguished himself as speaker of the lower house. Later he was chosen for the state supreme court. A long-time Democrat, he left his party because of the Fugitive Slave Act, joining the Free Soil Party in 1850 and, in 1854, the newly organized Republican Party. An outspoken opponent of slavery, Spalding donated his legal services in the Oberlin-Wellington rescue case as well as in the case of Lucy. In 1862 he was elected to Congress, representing Cleveland until 1868, during which time he helped draft important Reconstruction and financial legislation.

trict Judge. On her way to the Court a crowd of people had gathered near the Post-office building, in which the Court was held, and there was a great deal of excitement about the girl. One of the men in the crowd approached a colored man by the name of C. M. Richardson, who had been a resident of Cleveland for a number of years, and dealt Mr. Richardson a stunning blow on the head, which felled him to the ground. The man evidently thought that Mr. Richardson was there for the purpose of rescuing the girl. Another man in the crowd, an Irishman, stepped up to a colored man by the name of Munson, and raised a club and was about to strike him, when Hon. Jabez M. Fitch, who happened to be near, interposed, and prevented the threatened blow.

The girl was brought into the U. S. Court room, and before the hearing commenced, Mr. Ambush had some words with young Goshorn, right in the Court room, and pistols were drawn on both sides, but they were prevented from firing by the interposition of people in the Court room. After the trial the Judge ordered the girl to be delivered up to her master, who took her back with him to Wheeling, where she was placed in jail and severely punished.

One of the arguments among the people generally, why the girl should be given up was, that it might prevent rebellion on the part of the South, which perhaps is an indication of the sentiment then prevailing. The war, however, was sure to come, and was not the result of any wrangling over a captive female, as some of the wars we read of in history, but was founded upon sterner and nobler

81

principles. Not the fate of a single individual, but of a whole race, was involved in the great struggle which afterwards burst forth, and opened the flood-gates of liberty.

When the Union Army arrived in Wheeling, the girl was liberated, and her master, Mr. Goshorn, who had become a prisoner of war, was incarcerated in the same jail in which he had confined Lucy.

On the breaking out of the rebellion in 1861, the condition of the colored people was such, that not having the privilege of universal suffrage,[3] they had not the opportu-

[3] Ohio Negroes did not, of course, win full voting rights until the ratification of the Fifteenth Amendment in 1870 voided the statutes prohibiting Negro suffrage. Nonetheless, some Ohio Negroes had voted before that time, owing to a series of court decisions that admitted some mulattoes to the franchise. The application of this rule was, however, a subject of some confusion, because of the difficulty of defining just how white a "white man" had to be. This was not a moot question. Many Ohio Negroes were mulattoes, presenting an infinite gradation between black and white. In 1850 the U. S. Census listed 14,265 Ohio Negroes as mulattoes out of a total colored population of 25,279. Were all of these mulattoes "Negroes" in the legal sense? If not, where and how was the racial line to be drawn? The courts grappled with this problem for years. In 1831 they ruled that any man "of race nearer white than mulatto" was entitled to vote. In 1834, in a case involving public education, "white" was defined as a matter of ancestry rather than color of skin, and further decisions permitted all those whose ancestry was more than one-half white to enjoy the legal position of white men. In 1859 the Ohio Supreme Court reversed this trend, depriving all mulattoes of the right to enter public schools, and in that same year the legislature withdrew the franchise from any person with "a distinct and visible admixture of African

82

nity to exercise a very wide or extended influence upon the living question which then agitated the country, and, as a consequence, they were left almost powerless to organize or do anything in co-operation with the white people towards the suppression of the rebellion, or towards the emancipation of their race. Nevertheless, there were a great many white citizens who were deeply in sympathy with the colored race.

On the election of Mr. Lincoln as President, the Republican party made very rapid strides towards its present strength and unity, and many of the citizens of Cleveland, among whom I might mention Hon. D. R. Tilden, John Huntington, W[illia]m. P. Fogg, Hon. Sherlock J. Andrews, Hon. R. F. Payne, Charles Stetson, Esq., John A. Foot, Esq., J. M. Hoyt, Esq., Edward Wade, Esq., George A. Benedict, Edwin Cowles, Rev. Dr. Aiken, Rev. Levi Tucker, M. C. Younglove, Richard C. Parsons, and many others, were active Republicans at the time, and took an earnest part in all the deliberations of the Republican party.

Whenever the colored people made any movement, or needed any advice, they consulted with these respective gentlemen. The Rev. Dr. Aiken[4] especially, interested him-

---

blood," giving the local election officials the authority to reject anyone with a Negro appearance. On the eve of the Civil War, therefore, Ohio had succeeded in disenfranchising those few Negroes who could vote and this arrangement continued throughout the entire Civil War and much of the Reconstruction era.

[4] Samuel C. Aiken (1791-1879) was the first pastor of Cleveland's First Presbyterian Church. Although he frequently used his pul-

self in behalf of the condition of the colored people. Long before, when the fugitive slave law was being passed, at a meeting held at the First Presbyterian Church, of which he was the pastor, he strongly denounced that law, and expressed sentiments in favor of resisting its enforcement. At that meeting it was resolved, that in case of the arrest of a fugitive slave, the church bells of the city should be rung as notice to the people of the arrest. Mr. M. C. Younglove offered a reward of five dollars to the sexton who should on such an occasion ring the first bell. Rev. Dr. Aiken afterwards proved to be a powerful friend to the colored people, and aided them by his counsel in their deliberations.

When the rebellion first broke out, I undertook to have a meeting called of the colored people of Cleveland, and, in conjunction with others, a meeting was called at the National Hall, on the Public Square.[5] It was proposed at that meeting that the colored people of Cleveland should organize military companies to assist in putting down the rebel-

---

pit as a forum to urge the repeal of the Black Laws, Aiken had the reputation, in some quarters, as a moderate on the slavery question. In 1858, however, at a meeting of the Presbyterian General Assembly held in Cleveland, Aiken, in a moving speech, denounced slavery as a monstrous evil. These sentiments, coming from a man with his reputation, helped convince southern delegates of the uniform hostility of northern Presbyterians and helped precipitate the division of the church into northern and southern wings, thus snapping one more thread that had bound the Union together.

[5] The meeting was held October 11, 1861, at National Hall. Joseph Williams presided, and Malvin was listed as a member of the committee.

lion, and it was also proposed that an application should be made to the Governor[6] for that purpose. But when the committee delegated for that purpose laid our request before the Governor, he declined to accept it, giving as a reason, that the matter was in the hands of the white people, and that they would take care of it. When Governor Brough was elected, a similar meeting was called, and another application for the same purpose was made to Governor Brough, but with no better result. In some of the New England States however, they had permitted colored companies to be formed, and many of the colored men of Cleveland left Ohio and went to Massachusetts, and joined colored regiments there formed, among others, W[illia]m. Underhill, John Brown, and Charles Brown, sons of John Brown, (otherwise known as John Brown, the barber,) Joseph Richardson and Benjamin Richardson, and others. Shortly afterwards the proclamation of emancipation was issued, and then it was that colored companies began to organize in Ohio, and from that time on, the influence of the colored people became more powerful. The resistance at that time of the leading copperheads was very bitter, and a strong aversion and repugnance was manifested by many of them against the colored people taking part in public affairs. The prejudice then existing, and which I suppose existed in every similar instance in history, where a people who have been looked upon as a despised race, and have risen above the condition in which they have been placed by

---

[6] William Dennison.

85

unfortunate circumstances, has pretty well worn away in the Northern States, and it is not strange to see a colored man propose measures in common with his white fellow-citizens for the common weal and benefit of all. Distinctions which are founded on human policy, without reference to the divine or natural law, and which tend to the degradation of a set of human beings, cannot be lasting, and must sooner or later succumb to the dictates of reason and humanity. Would this were accomplished in the Southern States. There intimidation and threats make the life of the colored man a thousand times more miserable than the worst condition of bondage. But as right will sooner or later prevail, the day will come when another nemesis will overtake and destroy the evil at the South.

It has been demonstrated that an intelligent colored man can be as good a citizen as an intelligent white man, and the same reasoning will hold good between an ignorant colored man and an ignorant white man.

I am now eighty-three years of age, and I thank God that he has spared my life long enough to witness the change wrought in the condition of the colored people. We read of the miraculous deliverance of the Israelites from bondage. It seems hardly less than a miracle that has been the means of unloosening the shackles of the colored man. I firmly believe it to be the interposition of Divine Providence wrought through the instrumentality of the Republican party.

In conclusion, I can only say as did Simeon of old, when he saw the promised Messiah, "Now, Lord, lettest thou thy servant depart in peace according to thy Word, for mine eyes have seen thy salvation."

Index